in a slant light

cilla mcqueen

in a slant light

a poet's memoir

OTAGO

Published by Otago University Press
Level 1, 398 Cumberland Street
Dunedin, New Zealand
university.press@otago.ac.nz
www.otago.ac.nz/press

First published 2016

ISBN 978-1-877578-71-7

Published with the assistance of Creative New Zealand

Editor: Emma Neale
Design/layout: Fiona Moffat
Author photograph: Libby Furr

Front cover: Cilla McQueen, *Self Portrait*, 1991. Ink drawing on paper, 298 x 210mm.
Hocken Collections, Te Uare Taoka o Hākena, Dunedin.

Printed in China through Asia Pacific Offset Ltd

1949

On 22 January in Birmingham, England, after an arduous birth
I opened my eyes and looked around.
The nurse remarked, 'She has been here before.'
I was a newborn point of view.

~

The first inscription in my consciousness
crisp cloth against my cheek, being held up to a window
to see snowflakes whirling softly in the darkness
drifting down beyond the frame, lit from inside the room
where I was lifted up to see this loveliness.
The word was spoken with delight.

~

My Australian father loved the snow, as he loved my English mother.
This memory must date from my first six months in England, before we
moved to Brisbane; I saw no more snow until I was four, our first winter
in Dunedin. Dad took us up Flagstaff and we slid on tea-trays down a
field. On his rectangular tray, my brother Malcolm went down straight
and fast; my tray was round and I was lighter, descended in wild circles
and fell off.

~

Snaps, tableaux – can't be sure about the authenticity of memory,
but by my lights it's all I have to go on.
Light, then voices, scent of fresh linen, snowflakes falling.

~

During the War Ewen Garth, a naval surgeon, met a Wren, Marion
Constance, who vowed to follow him to the ends of the earth, even to
the Antipodes, and be faithful forever. Their love was a beacon. Singing
together made them cry.
Half a century later, watching him from the kitchen window

as he pushed the mower on the back lawn,
stopping to mop his forehead with a handkerchief,
she said, 'When we die, we'll be Baucis and Philemon,
I hope, turn into trees.'

~

In Brisbane
my fingertips
touch dancing motes
in a slant sunbeam.
On the other hand, she told me,
Mum in the doorway
saw me stretching up my arms
to two giant spiders, just beyond my reach.

~

Soft feet at the beginning of summer
skirt dangers; poisonous snakes in the gully,
spiders in the Thunderbox that might climb up
and bite your bottom.

Mum lies on a tartan rug
guarding the thermos and sandwiches,
ham and tomato, with the other mothers
reclining like kangaroos
under the trees in the blinding shadow,
while Dad sculpts racing cars of sand
with driftwood wheels and seaweed dashboard,
cool deep driving seat.

My deckchair and sunhat in the garden, my solitude.

On Guy Fawkes night so quick and light
I run towards the bonfire as fast as I can –
strong arms grab me, swing me high

in my primrose dress with a heart-shaped pocket,
puffed sleeves, pearly smocking across the chest.
I write on the night sky with a sparkler.

The feel of silk stored in my nerves –
a dress the colour of wild lupins, I'd say now –
at that time more familiar were red earth,
misty bluegums, streaky bark, dark bush
in the gully beyond the chicken run
where the orphaned joey lived.
His mother was blinded by the headlights.
Dad brought him home – early morning surprise –
the joey thumping, black poos scattering on the floor.
He lived with the bantams.
I gazed into the distance in his eyes.
When he grew large we gave him to the zoo.

~

Bushfire smoke-scent, taste of sugar cane,
scent of rainforest paths, the scent of rain
on cool wide leaves, sun piercing shade.
A fireball rolling down the road like thistledown.

Prickly tobacco scent in Dad's tweed sportscoat,
black with green flecks, plaited leather buttons.
I believed that I saw smoke-rings puffing out his ears.

~

In the large lead shoe X-ray machine
at the back of the shoe shop, our skeletal
feet appeared at the press of a button.
We irradiated ourselves further
when the shop assistant wasn't looking.

I tried the magic trick of pulling the tablecloth out
from under our plates of tomato soup. This didn't work.
My brother taught me new words, explained things,
went ahead, made the way safe.

He gallantly climbed the pantry shelves to reach
a jar of golden syrup, but the lid came off.
To this day he bends my ear on quantum physics.

~

We had two grandmothers to love:
Australian Florence and English Muriel,
whose scents were lavender and fresh linen.

When Granny came from England
I drove with her in the open air
in the rumble seat of Fanny Ford.

Red and green curtains, port and starboard,
in the room where she slept in a pure white nightie,
her hair pure white too. We jumped into her warm bed
in the morning and she read to us,
If Jesus Came to My House
and *When We Were Very Young*.
Then she was gone.

She had a musical voice like Mum's,
who missed her mother all her life.
Handwritten airmail letters between them flew
around the world for decades,
landing in our letterbox, blue doves.

~

I named my doll Rosebug.
Bug sounded cosy, snug in the rug of a rose.

I cried at *Blinky Bill*'s very sad chapter.
Shy the Platypus. Every night a story, prayers,
Goodnight God Bless Amen.

My straight brown hair, my hair ribbon.
The bobby pin has one leg straight,
the other kinked,
shiny brown shoes on metal feet, nice to
delicately bite.

1953

Our sister Alison has flaxen hair.
Her christening robe exceeds her baby legs.
My new doll is Felicity, my friend at kindergarten Maurice.

~

Leaving for New Zealand on a Sunderland flying boat,
I am sick in the gutter. Then our departure is delayed;
the plane unloaded and reloaded because Felicity,
in the luggage, mewed like a cat.

All the bright burin writes in me –

Brilliant white spray dashed across the porthole
as we land in Wellington Harbour.
My first sight of Aotearoa.

~

Dad's work is at the medical school. At first we live in a university house,
a half-timbered villa at the corner of Union and Cumberland Streets.
I think J.K. Baxter and his family also lived there, years later.

~

The second house, 20 Leven Street, is two-storeyed
with steep stairs and long smooth banisters.
In a cupboard I find a long-playing record
and score around it with a pin,
which makes an interesting music.

The man next door has seedling trays
arranged in the sun on his side of the fence.
I climb up and look over, see rows of soft green shoots.
I pull one out – it makes a 'plick' –
pull out the whole tray one by one.

He tells Mum and she tells Dad
who speaks severely. I confess,
I did lean over the fence, I did
plick all those little seedlings out
of their yielding soil one by one,
because I liked the sound.

1954

Five years old on the front doorstep,
ready for school on a bright blue morning.
I walk right around the house, discover
to my satisfaction that there is indeed
not a cloud in the sky.

~

Arthur Street School. My brother's there already among the big boys.
Stiff new brown satchel, straps and buckles, lunch in a brown paper
bag, new pencil case.

Belinda has fair curly hair, a red and white gingham dress. She
introduces me to Juliet, Gretchen, Vicky, Helen:
so many people in the class I'm shy.

Primer One has high windows, opened by our teacher
with a long pole, a slur-shaped metal hook at the end.
In the centre of the room is a pot-bellied stove
where she makes cocoa for us on cold mornings.
At first we print with a disappointingly thin grey
pencil on a slate.

~

I want to learn to read.
Janet and John has large black print;
I discover a facility in recognition
of the letter and its sound, that clarity
of type on paper like the sharpness
at the edge of sleep, as large and clear
as the edge of the doorway,
corner of the bedroom ceiling,
pink wallpaper popped in the corners
as far up as I can reach.

Janet and John, Hansel and Gretel –
in the forest of letters appears
a magical opening, a clearing
where at last the twiggy print
resolves in sounding words.

~

Learning to Read

I remember the look
of the unreadable page

the difficult jumble

and then the page
became transparent

and then the page
ceased to exist:

at last I was riding this bicycle
all by myself.

~

Dad brings Mum a cup of tea in bed.
I snuggle in to her warmth.
When she lifts her cup, her diamond ring
sets Tinkerbells dancing on the ceiling.
As I move my head, spectral colours
flash around the mirror's bevelled edge.

1955

Our new address is 5 Hart Street. At the Ross Street end, Mackay's Store occupies one corner. On the other corner there's a whispery silver birch tree. Dawdle up to get the bread for Mum; coming back, taste feather by feather its warm white middle till it's hollow as a nest.

A green wooden gate. A white villa with a green roof, steps up to the porch, front door opening into the hall, drawing room to the right, Mum and Dad to the left, bedrooms either side, dining room in the middle,

kitchen, pantry, bathroom at the back. A Shacklock range and a gas
stove where Dad makes porridge every morning.
A green Formica kitchen table.

Outside the back door is the wash-house with cobwebs, double concrete
tubs, washing machine, wringer, old copper in its brick surround. Bluo.
Concrete steps up to the washing line. Red currants, blackcurrants,
white currants, gooseberries in the vegetable garden at the top of the
slope. It takes a long time to pick enough fruit for blackcurrant jam
or a fool.

~

Pink-cheeked, in dark blue corduroy overalls,
fair Alison among the daffodils.
'A host,' says Mum. 'It is a host of dancing daffodils.'

~

Under the rhododendrons there's a tunnel
where we thread the pink and purple flowers on flax
to make garlands, the petals soft and moist.

~

A frosty winter morning, walking down
the hill to school past city council workmen
at the junction of Ross Street and City Road
around their brazier with holes in its metal sides,
brilliant points of fire. Steaming breath of the cheerful workmen
stamping their feet, cupping tin mugs in their hands.

Down City Road, long black skid-marks in the frost.
Schoolbag, reading books, exercise book, lunchbox,
pencil case. My Black Beauty's shining barrel
with silver lettering engraved – the bliss
of making pencil marks on paper – birds on sky –
first stroke of a sharpened lead

on the silken surface of the opening page,
first line of a brand new exercise book.

~

Dreaming aqua horizons, dawn-red margin.
Over and over print rows of lettering
never neat enough; erase until a hole appears,
the page is ruined, tear it out and start again.
Some of my exercise books are thin, especially arithmetic.

~

At the edge of the playground
we play bumblebee telephones.
Place a handkerchief over
a bumblebee sitting on a dahlia
and hold it tight
around the stem.
It buzzes.
Ring ring, ring ring,
you hold it to your ear
or your friend's ear
(but not too close).

~

Doll alarm, hard work with rubber bands and hooks
holding Felicity's arms and legs on.
Her lashless eyes have rolled back in her head.
At the Dolls Hospital she gets new eyes
and crimped blonde hair.
I open my birthday present and find
immaculate Jemima in a Pedigree box.

Small girls are likely to be squashed
playing 'more on still, stacks on the mill'.

A boy has his mouth washed out with soap
in the concrete drinking trough, for bad language.

~

On Saturday mornings we walk down the hill
to the Children's Library in Stuart Street.
At the top of the entrance stairs with polished banisters,
a cubby-hole for returning books
to Mrs Dorothy White, the librarian.
At the other end of the library, the Exit stairs
are a mirror image of the entrance.

The stamp on the end of the librarian's pencil,
with which she impresses in ink the date
at the front of the book and on my library card,
reminds me of a hammerhead shark.

~

I like spelling and vocabulary, am annoyed when 'fatigue' and
'physician' trip me up.

~

Bronze penny fills my hand,
silver threepence as thin as a moon.
Farthings are remembered by the shopkeeper
of the triangular dairy, its door on the corner
of York Place and Rattray Street.
I come in to the widening space, approach
the glass counter, the sweets in bottles and trays
all shapes and colours, pink cachous, sherbet,
licorice, acid drops, pineapple chunks,
aniseed balls, a paper twist for a halfpenny.
Rainbow gobstoppers.
Once I got the strap. It hurt my hand.
The strap made the big boys boast.

~

As I write it seems some spry thing's yielding rapid-fire recollections,
leafing through each memory that can open, surrounded by adjacent
images ready to be sparked.
Too long untouched – keys rust – here comes our family's A40,
Annie Austin, colour oyster.

School milk-bottle crate under the tree, out of the sun.
An apple a day or Bertie Germ will eat your teeth.
At the far corner of the playground
at the top of the steps near Boys' High
is the Murder House. Random people are called out
to meet the dental nurse's treadle drill.

~

Fifi, our springer spaniel,
has velvet ears and deep brown eyes full of longing.

~

On a clear night, a sound I associate with the edge of sleep
when ears are listening to faraway sounds,
steam engines shunting in the Hillside railway yards
in South Dunedin,
Tscha … Tscha … Tscha … Tscha … Tscha … Tschachachachachacha

~

Little Bo Peep, her porcelain face unchanged,
sits on my dressing table to this day.
A birthday present from Uncle Frank, my godfather,
she has lost only her silver-buckled black felt shoes
and her shepherdess's crook. She still wears her straw bonnet
with ribbon, dress and flowery overskirt,
petticoat and lace-edged underwear.
Her hair is fair and fine, her eyes forget-me-not.
Her innocence endures.

18

My last doll was tall Muriel.
Her long legs hinged at the hip.

~

I discovered with surprise that my mother spoke French. My first
French word was *la fenêtre*, more mysterious than an ordinary window.

~

White porcelain inkwells
in the right-hand corner of the wooden desks.
The solemn ink monitor pours blue ink
from a long-necked jug, a little into each.

The nib is more demanding than the pencil.
It will dig in and make a blot, require the blotter.
The spidery handwriting takes shape
in repetitious exercises to perfect each letter,
my page not neat; frequently the nib will cross,
sully the white paper,
which has different tactile qualities
recto to verso, as silk to satin.

~

Impossible to buy a pie
at the counter of the tuck-shop in Arthur Street
when the Boys' High boys charge in.

~

I rhyme the Municipal Baths in Moray Place
with Runcible Spoon.
The air is full of echoing shrieks.
Malcolm dives fearlessly from the high board.
At last, the faith to jump – Dad catches me,
teaches me to float, a curious feeling.
Sunday breakfast, lamb's fry and bacon, fried bread, tomato sauce.

~

I say goodbye to my best friend Belinda
at the bus stop, tell her I'll miss her.
Her serious blue eyes – she says,
'No you won't.'

1956

Ocean liner looming, her bow like a black nib above the wharf where
Dad waves us goodbye. Brave Mum is taking me, Malcolm and Alison
to England for six months to visit Granny. The paper streamers stretch
and snap, wind and waves take them.

The caulked deck scrubbed white, rope quoits, deckchairs, interesting
maze of companionways and cabins, polished wood and brass. The
Purser and the Shop, our cabin, porthole, stewardess in white uniform.

In the dining room our table and our waiter, a printed menu every day,
elaborate cutlery, serviettes; we have to watch our manners.

I learn to swim – just as well – when we Cross the Line:
burly sailor-mermaids with rope-seaweed hair
slather all the children in green ice-cream and throw us
in the swimming pool.
We receive a certificate signed by Neptune.

Malcolm tells me what appalling depth of ocean
our ship, which seems so safe, is floating on.

Tall mirrors between bookcases, books restrained against the roll. In
the ship's library we do our homework for the Correspondence School.

Hushed atmosphere of the polished stateroom, deep hum of engines,
ocean all around. A place for concentration.

Our ship's peculiar stasis in the Panama Canal.

~

My interest in opposites began at the Equator when our ship
passed through a *Door That Wasn't There* from southern to northern
hemisphere, some imaginary meniscus like that between the mirror
image staircases at the Children's Library, or *Through the Looking Glass.*

~

Into, for instance, England, land of my mother,
the War and Buckingham Palace. As English
as my aunts, thatched cottages, afternoon tea
at a Lyons tea-house, fine china,
tiered trays of *petits fours.*

Everything the same as home but rather warped,
like the voices of familiar-unfamiliar cousins
in front of a stately-looking home
playing croquet on the lawn.

Muriel, the widow of the Rev. Going,
lives at Traveston, Sutton Road, Shrewsbury.
White hair, navy blue crêpe dress
swinging seat in the kitchen garden,
ripe plums underfoot, wasps in the plums.

Shrewsbury, the curious taste of quince.
I visit Granny's neighbour, Mrs Seabrook,
in whose quiet drawing room the sun
through leadlight windows casts a sheen
on a small mahogany table,
her magnifying glass lying on it.

Crossing the road, 'Priscilla!
If you run ahead of me I shall be vexed.'
That word stopped me.
It was new in my vocabulary.
I heard and saw the *x* at the centre of the word,
graven deeper by the situation,
my crossing the road ahead of my grandmother.

~

Standing on the railway bridge when the train roars underneath will
cover you in soot.
Mum hoped her mother wouldn't find us wild colonial children. There
was a contrast between English manners and the alien etiquette of the
Antipodes. We weren't rowdy but we had New Zealand accents, a sense
of home elsewhere. There seemed some challenge in 'Antipodes', an
opposition, answering back, something contrary, even disobedient.

Antiphonal. Antimatter.
Indeed it was thought that we were upside down,
observing Christmas in midsummer

New Zealand's trees were always green;
regrettably there was not the play of seasons –
England was the template – meadow flowers,
Pooh-sticks in the stream, cobblestones,
stone churches, silver teaspoons.

It was six months' hard work for Mum with all three children, missing
Dad, but we were busy visiting the family here and there, meeting our
cousins and aunts but not our Uncle Philip, who was killed in Italy in
the War.

A new dress, pink muslin sprigged with blue flowers.
Covent Garden's chandeliers and evening dress
as dazzling as the ballets that we watch

with Uncle Frank of Montagu Square, from
a box – funny idea – *Swan Lake* and *Les Sylphides*.

~

Home on the *Orontes*.
Suez – scarabs, a silver bracelet.
A magician comes aboard at Aden
wearing a red fez. Beaming, he doffs it,
revealing an identical fez
and another and another.
Setting these four fez on a table
like upturned flower pots,
he mysteriously produces
from underneath each one
a yellow chicken.

~

At the wharf in Sydney, Dad's standing on the railing, waving wildly,
red-faced, in a grey suit. We see Mum and Dad kissing. Dad shuts the
door, laughing.

My grandmother Florence is small and neat, with glasses,
a floral dress, red lipstick.
She kisses me – tiny lines all around her mouth.

G'Pa looks like Dad, but sterner. He lets me ride the scooter.
I scoot down the winding path through flickering shadows
to the Old Cremorne wharf, push it uphill, scoot down again
with my heel on the brake, in control.

~

G'Pa's doctoral thesis in education was *The Distribution of Attention*.
Innovative educator, he was headmaster of Pymble Ladies' College
before he took up medicine. Florence and he were married in 1914. They
spent their honeymoon in Edinburgh. On the way back to London,

she told me, their train grew ever longer as it stopped at all the stations,
picking up young soldiers off to the trenches of World War I.

~

Lyttelton to Dunedin, the sliding, clanging plates between the carriages.
Lunch at Oamaru, coming off the train in a crowd of people in overcoats,
taking a place at a long table with white tablecloths and stiff serviettes.
Red-brown tea in a cup as heavy as stone.
Boiling hot soup to be eaten very fast
or be left behind when everyone rushes back to the train.
Tunnels, close the window
or you get black nostrils.

Back at No 5, I am too chic
with my shoulder bag, striped dress, bobby socks.
Belinda is there
but Muriel is missing.
There is no Fifi.
And oh, my English accent sets me apart.
At Arthur Street I'm now a Pommie Brainbox
and Four-Eyes, to boot.

1957

At the front door of 5 Hart Street
my new lenses see clear across the road,
each branch, twig, serrated leaf,
the intricate edges of a tree.
I didn't know I was short-sighted
till I couldn't read the blackboard.
When I take the glasses off
trees blur to felted blots.

I put them on again for good,
trade the wind on my eyelids
for focus in a frame.

Our family has no extended family to know or be known by, or to show
us how to talk. Pommie puzzles me. I sound normal from inside.

I refuse to wear the box-pleated
grey flannel divided skirt, a present
from an aunt. In case you show
your underwear, doing cartwheels?
Along with my stuck-up voice
it chafes. The time I wore it
some girls whispered.
Self-consciousness froze me.

Bright lights, costumes, lipstick,
immense daring of going on stage
as Buttercup in *HMS Pinafore*.

I hope to be a ballerina.
Mum sews my ballet costumes on the Singer
with its complicated threading, shapely black body,
gold lettering, sensitive knee-pedal, smooth
mechanical chatter, housed in an arched
wooden case like a train in a tunnel.

In a green and orange shot-satin leotard
I dance; an iridescent dragonfly, feeling like
the Arthur Rackham illustrations of *Undine*;
and as Cinderella's coachman become a Rat
in grey satin with a grey rat-cap, red pipe-cleaner
whiskers. Light as whipped egg-white,
how desirable a crisp tutu!
Anna Pavlova has a lovely name.

Soft pink ballet shoes, glossy ribbons
crossed over the arch of my foot.

~

Quick minds mesh like music
in flurries of invention
... *what say* ...
for dress-ups there are some dresses, a coat,
a pink satin ballgown, pink satin petticoat,
other petticoats, two evening stoles,
one with delicate silver thread embroidery,
a clutch of handbags, high heels, ladies' felt hats
with artificial flowers, a beret, a man's hat,
a pipe cleaner tiara furry with tinsel,
a sportscoat with very long arms
to be worn with a burnt cork moustache.
Imagination flies through sequences of scenes
as in a dream, or a Buñuel film.

~

A bulging satchel, closed with leather straps and two brass buckles,
the softened straps curled up at the ends. Exercise books, pencil case,
lunchbox, sandwiches often soggy, Marmite and tomato, not worth
swapping.

Finished all the reading books. Mr Grant lets me choose one from the
tall, varnished cupboards at the back of the classroom. Like a draught
of adult liquor, *Oliver Twist* has a profound effect on my world-view. At
eight, I'm young for such insight into human nature.

~

With my head on the pillow, I listen to rhythm
in ballads of limitless courage. Dad reads to us with gusto,
'The Highwayman', 'The Inchcape Rock',
'How Horatius Held the Bridge',

'The Charge of the Light Brigade',
'The Ballad of the Revenge' – curiously,
Mum's Sir Richard – then five minutes of reading
our library books until lights out.
Goodnight God Bless Amen.

Matching berets and coats with a velvet collar,
Ali's blue, mine dark red.
My hair is mouse, Ali's gold, her forehead
blessed with a cow-lick.

Mistake: take Mum's new lipstick to school
put it on
but it won't wash off
have to go home with a red mouth.

Deciding to be a circus acrobat
I know exactly how to walk
the tightrope we've strung up in the old workshop,
step out with confidence, fall flat on my back.

~

At Sunday school it's hard to colour neatly inside the lines of the Bible
story pictures in my workbook. Our vicar has a sense of humour;
one day from the pulpit he produces a live hen.

Intriguing parables
layers of meaning
light streaming into the nave
vermilion and cobalt glass
high choirboy voices
stone acoustics.

~

For birthday parties we have as usual hundreds and thousands on triangles of white bread and cheerios with tomato sauce. I can eat a large number of cheerios; am told to hold back. Mum and Dad direct the games, Musical Chairs, Statues, Musical Bumps, General Post, Oranges and Lemons, making Amazing Hats out of newspaper, Pin the Tail on the Donkey, or else we're blindfolded and given a selection of things to identify by smell, like vanilla, shoe-polish, peanut butter, Marmite, soap, or asked to memorise a number of articles on a tray briefly seen and whipped away, then write them down.

~

Writing stories in cut-in-half exercise books,
my hand more fluent page by page,
as much for the joy of writing as for the plot,
usually magic or horses –
the inky nib transcribing thoughts
unfolding like a game – keeping the whole in mind
but not the end – then you run out of pages.

Home from school with chickenpox,
listening to *Portia Faces Life* and Aunt Daisy
on the Sharp transistor radio that Dad brought back
from Hong Kong, I'm more interested in
my invisible drawing book's smooth paper,
its hidden lines discovered by my pencil
and my invisible painting book, painted
with plain water – as the wet brush passes over
the page thrills into colour.

Dry black stuff in a cellophane packet
blooms in a glass of water overnight
cyan, chrome, lime green, hot pink,
Hong Kong Magic Flowers.

~

The Children's Holiday Programme runs competitions in close listening,
identifying sound and detail, a snippet of sound from everyday life
played fast or slow: washing machine, squeaky hinge, kettle, can opener.

Eyes closed in concentration at the kitchen table we listen to the
evening serials *Life with Dexter*, *Night Beat*, *Journey into Space*,
imaginary worlds as rich as Dickens's.

~

Although the cable cars up Rattray Street
are gone, like farthings, clay cuttings remain.
Walking home from school we short-cut
up a bank under silver birch and cross the sports field,
Robin Hood. But if we hear before we see
the rugby thundering, we walk around the edge.

~

Cardboard tube, paper twist, spitting stars,
rocket in a milk bottle, stand back, stand back!
Wake up early and climb out the window.
The morning air still holds a tinge of gunpowder.
Gather spent Emerald Fire, Golden Rain, Vesuvius,
Bengal Light, Jumping Jack, bent sparkler wires,
memories of brilliance from the dewy grass
my bare footprints dark green.

1958

Beside Lake Wakatipu in a canvas tent
on a stormy night, I fall asleep listening
to the wind's orchestra.
Blink, wake

to perfect morning reflections:
gold, aquamarine, cerulean
dazzle.

Along the dusty road to the one-lane wooden bridge
over the Kawarau, along the dusty road across the flats
to the garage at the Frankton corner, to fill our billy
with fresh milk ladled from the churn. Please hold
the returning billy sensitively by its wire handle,
lest it slop.

We take jam jars up to the frog pond to catch tadpoles
among the bullrushes and dragonflies,
set them by the bed in hope of finding
a frog in the morning, or a prince.

Of this hillside beside the lake we know no history – history at school
being concerned with the northern hemisphere – to us, this land was
bare before we came, a childhood *terra nullius*.

~

To celebrate the homecoming to No 5
of Mum and our new sister Fiona,
we decide to make a two-tone jelly.
We make the Greggs green jelly; leave it to set
in a Pyrex dish, then make the red jelly
and pour it on top. But the red is too hot
and melts the green,
turning it all
one brown.
When this plain brown jelly is set
we try to turn it out but it is stuck
so I hold it upside down over the sink
and turn the the hot tap on.
The jelly flops out in one piece,

breaks up and slithers down the plughole.
We scrabble for jelly while Dad breaks his meringues
off the walls of the oven with a hammer.

~

In conversation
my new baby sister
gurgles and kicks,
watching me talk.
I look into her eyes,
see she understands.
The mind in there
connects with mine.

~

At Helen's place we play in a sunroom
up a staircase with a curtain at the bottom,
daylight prickling through dark red chenille.
Behind this curtain, on a table, is a typewriter –
not supposed to be touched
but I can hardly tear myself away
for fascination with the letters
appearing on the blank sheet
representing language, meaning – mistakes –
the incongruity of this serious machine
in my inexpert hands creating nonsense
as it casts up inky letters one by one.

The metal arms whack black on white,
the daddy-long-legs twist, jam, lock.
It makes me laugh aloud.

1959

Dark-framed glasses, dark hair, his green jersey knitted by Aunt Norah.
In Malcolm's room are Spitfires and Mosquitoes suspended from the
ceiling, sheets of balsa wood, razor blades, pottles of coloured aeroplane
dope, bright copper wires, transistors, glowing valves, soldering iron,
sudden shouts of warning.

He's built a crystal set on which we listen to *The Goon Show*,
the sort of wit Dad chuckles over, handing *Punch* to Mum.

On the back lawn we make up a game
of gabbling in unison in Goon-type voices
tripping over the edge of sense, bursting into laughter
at the sound and look of words
turning peculiar when the rules break.

As with the fascinating typewriter
my sense of humour enjoys instabilities,
chance juxtapositions rendering meaning
unstable – until the language wobbles,
turns into nonsense – for instance
how many times can you say 'people' all on one breath
in different voices?

Later, I amuse myself making musical scores, with printed letters in
the mind evoking imaginary voices – a room full of people chattering,
whispering, exclaiming.
Intervals of silence.

~

At school it is hilarious when everyone
has to call out their middle name.
Mine's embarrassing, Muriel,
prim *u* and dotted *i* like a string of pearls,
an Englishness I'd rather hide, to be the same.

Each in our place. 'Children,' says Mum, 'should be seen and not heard,' but she doesn't really mean it. The family eats and talks. Cutlery, serviette rings; one sets the table, another clears away, all of us help with the washing up.
Mum sits by the Conray heater,
Dad commandeers the sink. No squabbling.

~

Books and radio are all – we see what we hear, minds fed by words and music. I am swallowed by the cinema, my vision of a fairy story witch scarily contradicted by the sight of Disney's adult witch in *The Sleeping Beauty*, the nightmare blandness of cartoon.

~

I'm not cut out to be a ballerina,
not like the Russian ones whose arabesque
is nearly the splits, but I can do mime.
The ballet studio of graceful Moira Hayes,
with wide polished floor and mirrors,
is at the top of the old Exchange building
in the centre of Dunedin – Victorian;
grass and toetoe growing in the guttering
among the gargoyles – I think there were gargoyles –

Giselle, *The Sleeping Beauty*, *Petrouchka*,
The Nutcracker, *Coppelia*; I learn the music of my LPs
by heart, spend my pocket money in Arthur Barnett's
on a yard of sea-green chiffon
to dance with when I portray the wind
in a ballet we perform in the dining room
with blankets for curtains.
Before the performance there's a solemn hush,
commitment to the music.

Our ballet class is invited to take part
in a Music Department production of *Venus and Adonis*.
In silver tunics fastened at one shoulder
we cherubs cluster around Honor McKellar
as Venus; draped in white, her blonde hair upswept.
My body feels the rippling soundwaves of her voice.

~

Somebody is usually sick on the way
to Frankton, in the Kawarau Gorge
whose thin road follows every bluff.
'Green Grow the Rushes O'
sings the family in the car
past Roaring Meg the power station;
Gentle Annie tumbling down
into the Kawarau, past tawny tussock,
bracken, rosehip, fences, boulders, weeping willow
turning up sheep-nibbled fingertips
in the rocky gorge that opens
into shining flats and goldrush tailings;
the Remarkables; at last Lake Wakatipu.

On the sloping section above the beach, two huts.
A white hut with three bunks up one wall,
a mattress on the floor for Mum and Dad,
Fio's cot. We listen to Dad snore.
A brown hut with a wood-burning stove,
a wire rack for drying socks and mittens.

The Tilly meticulously lit, the fuel ejector
pricked, the lamp pumped up at speed
until the cloth bulb blooms to hissing brilliance,
illuminates the hut where we play
Scrabble and Monopoly.

Lizards, frog pond, bullrushes – vanished now – the spirit of the place has gone suburban. Perhaps we had the best of it, those young summers without jet engines in the air or on the lake, bare land all the way to Kelvin Grove, a few holiday cribs; a privilege to have known the natural beauty of that hill before it was turned to use.

1960

Mum, MA Oxon. with her perfect French, takes a teaching job at Columba College. Ali and I change schools suddenly. Nervous, new, I'm bumped up a year into Form 2.
Long corridors of gleaming red linoleum lined with book cupboards, green girls stampeding, imperative bells. Mysteries of the suspender belt.
I miss my friends at Arthur Street.

Nicknamed greengages, we walk
to town or church in crocodiles, two by two.
Kilt, jacket, white blouse, hat, brown shoes,
stockings, gloves. Silver hat-badge,
the dove of Saint Columba.

~

Dad demolishes the old workshop and makes a volley-board
for us to practise tennis shots. Straight brown hair, studious glasses,
strained smile, new tennis racquet, new school uniform.
I'm uncertain, eleven.
As he takes the photo he exhorts me to look
as though I like playing tennis. Gaily dashing about
what ho, like English cousins.
I am no good at it, hold my racquet like a spoon,
tend to dodge the ball
for fear it will knock my glasses off.

~

Dislocated from my year-group, I'm shy. Miss Bell doesn't seem to like
our class. *Ridout* is our grammar book, clauses and phrases, particles
and articles hammered in.
I dread maths, make mistakes, feel gloomily it doesn't make sense. We
learn by heart and recite in unison Bracken's lugubrious
'Not Understood'.

~

Before we are allowed to cook, we have to sew
by hand, backstitch, with felled seams,
a white linen apron and cap. In red embroidery cotton
we must chain-stitch on the cap
our name in cursive writing.
By the time the others are making scones
I'm still slaving over my grubby handful of linen.
Priscilla is so lengthy to embroider –
I've never learned the ins and outs of scones.

~

In the wash-house in the evenings
Malcolm grinds a piece of porthole-glass
with carborundum, a lens for his telescope.
Tired of homework I go out
to learn about the universe.
He tells me about the solar system, comets, stars.
I wonder whether Infinity is God.

~

Long wooden skis and leather boots,
bamboo ski-poles, spring-and-wire
mousetrap bindings, unsteady
competence in the snow-plough.
Malcolm skis away from me at speed.
The rope tow scares me,

I can't master the nutcracker,
I am too small. When I go past a pulley
the rope falls off and drags heavily along the ground.
Every time a coconut, says the angry man following.

~

Early winter morning
bracken rosehip shingle
water stepping green to blue
below trout ripples intersecting
settling to glass
before the breeze gets up

~

My tartan kilt, heavy and warm, swings when I walk.
Handed secretly around the classroom, *Angélique* falls open at certain
pages. Innuendo is puzzling. The older girls have secrets; a year
younger than the others I'm anxious about periods and what to do.
Mum says 'Sex' in neon quotation marks.
I find an educational pamphlet, *Sex and the Adolescent Girl*, in the front
room and read it behind the sofa when she's out. It's coldly abstract –
I'm none the wiser.

~

At the Dental School, a student in orthodontics
does violence to my mouth. The solution
for my crowded upper jaw is deemed to be
the removal of two milk and two permanent teeth.
Anaesthetised in a gas mask I wake up laughing,
tasting blood. I have to wear a pink plastic
dental plate with a steel wire, supposed to correct
the bite, but instead it creates a diastema
between my two front teeth.
I mind this gap.

1961

We all go with Dad on sabbatical leave to Birmingham.
Six weeks on the *Rangitoto* – grown-up luxury –
I'm sitting in a deckchair at morning tea time
watching the waves when a smiling steward
in a white jacket appears, bearing on a tray
an ice-cold glass pearled with moisture
of prickly black Coca-Cola
with a parasol, a toothpick with a cherry,
a straw with a ruffled-up paper case.

For fancy dress I'm an Ocean Wave, white crêpe paper
cut in a frothy fringe, a long green crêpe-paper train.
Interesting English sweets in the shop:
Aero chocolate, Rowntrees Fruit Gums, Maltesers.
A necklace of purple seeds from Pitcairn Island,
a moonstone necklace from Peru.
Callao – Lima – Bermuda – Birmingham.
A homely feeling at 91 Oxford Road, Moseley.

~

Our school is Mum's old school,
Edgbaston Church of England College for Girls,
whose principal is our Aunt Marnie.

The winter uniform is mainly brown:
beret, jersey, skirt, cream blouse;
the summer uniform a gingham dress
in red, blue or green, with a white Panama hat.

At lunchtime in the dining room
we sit down at long tables, say grace,
wait till a bell is tinkled, eat without talking.
The best pudding is treacle tart and custard.

My friends think I have a funny accent.
I'm foreign again, the other way round.

In music lessons we listen to Bach, Bartók,
Mozart. Hearing melody and harmony
I spend ages setting the text
from Browning's 'Pippa's Song',
'The lark's on the wing/ the snail's on the thorn/
God's in his heaven/ All's right with the world';
hours in the art room with pen and ink
whispering verses of 'The Lady of Shalott',
drawing each stone of her castle, each whitening,
quivering leaf of willow and aspen.

Chain, double-chain, satin, feather, daisy.
In needlework we learn the stitches required
to work a sampler, demonstrate them
on the linen cover of a needle-case with white felt pages,
pinked edges, blue gingham lining,
initialled PM in blue cross-stitch.

It is the done thing to have a crush
on one of the serene, aloof prefects.

The whole school takes part in an open-air
historical pageant, in tableaux.
Dressed in Edwardian costume, our class sings
'Nymphs and Shepherds Come Away'
into a breeze that steals away our voices.

On a red double-decker bus
we travel home from school
through yellowish pea-soup fog.
Black nostrils.

~

At Aunt Marnie's house near St Agnes's vicarage
where the Going girls lived in childhood,
the garden path leads through a green gate
to the common. There's a pond with bullrushes,
winding paths, hummocky moss, leafy dells,
bluebells, a place to let imagination wander.
The sort of place, I think, for Hobbits.

~

Two sisters from next door
with lilting Birmingham accents
describe a Beatles concert
where everyone screamed so loud
you couldn't hear the Beatles.
They back-comb their hair into a bouffant beehive
which almost hides the school beret, folded
and pinned flat at the back of the head
like a burnt pancake.

~

We spend a summer week in Brittany
in a seaside hotel advertising
'*Fruits de Mer, Santé de Fer*'.
I speak some French, taste seafood,
crusty bread, café au lait, croissants,
swim in my new yellow bikini
the top of which is rather loose.
It is strictly forbidden to go into the sandhills
or near the old concrete bunkers
because there are German skeletons
left over from the War.

~

In late summer we move to a sixteenth-century farmhouse
near Evesham. Mum talks of battles, distinguished ancestors.
There's an orchard, a henhouse full of stinging nettles,
a sundial, a priest's hole, a closed-off wing,
a staircase glimpsed through a gap
in the boarded-up wall, three stray kittens,
an Aga stove on the vast flagstones of the kitchen floor.
Upstairs, a TV set. *The Black and White Minstrel Show*,
The Lone Ranger, the test pattern.
Frank Ifield sings 'I Remember Yoooooo'.

We drive to Birmingham with Dad to school and back. By winter, it's
dark when we leave home and dark when we return to the flagstoned
kitchen to do our homework in the warmth of the Aga, at the scrubbed
deal table, under the pots that hang on racks, like hats.

~

Smells of leather, saddle soap and horses.
Miss Gilbert runs a riding school. Dad rides Ginger,
I ride Kim, Ali rides Merrylegs, all in a collected way
through country lanes lined with hawthorn hedges.
One day Ginger bites me; his huge teeth
impress on my arm the cable-stitch of my jersey.

Trotting and cantering, learning to jump, then my riding stops abruptly
after a mishap that quenches my ballet aspirations and begins the long
story of my back, thereafter.

~

The Russian ballet teacher looks like a ballerina,
but older. Sharp black eyes, black hair
scraped back in a bun, she's brusque,
unlike the image of Anna Pavlova
in the *Girl's Book of Ballet*.

My spine is not bendy enough.
She is unhappy with my arabesque. Crossly
she places her hand under my thigh,
forces it upwards; I feel a gelatinous click
in the middle of my back, a soft, definite
displacement, gristle-shift, pain.

We wait to see if it improves –
it does – but by the age of thirty-six
I'll need a triple spinal fusion.

~

English winter; time to leave for home. Living for a week in the freezing
cold Palm Court Hotel, with crumbling gas fires, a shilling for the meter,
long corridors with ivy-covered-brick wallpaper, all of us except for Dad
get terrible flu. Having shepherded the family to the *Arcadia* he comes
down with it himself.

1962

Again a new girl at Columba,
fourth form, thirteen,
I find my place within
Moira-Bronwen-Lynn-Janet-Prue
a bright peer group
Carla-Jacqui-Primrose-Denise-Robyn
with a sense of humour
Claire-Noela-Mary-Andrea-Averil and all
in the same predicament,
growing up in the sixties,
decade of change.

Obediently we drink
our pink Salk polio vaccine
served in a miniature paper cup.

I'm indifferent in maths and science, ahead in Latin, History, English,
French.
Mum is our French teacher, for several decades on the Columba staff of
clever, independent women.

~

We move house to 23 Hart Street,
a villa with a sitting room and kitchen at the back,
a garden with trees and a flower bed
of pansy, snapdragon, aubretia, lobelia, viola, ixia.
Dad starts his endless task with the hand lawnmower,
snicka snicka snicka snicka on a Saturday morning,
wafting the scent of cut grass into my room
where I lie reading *Lorna Doone*.

~

Home has a comfortable atmosphere of fluent, affectionate
conversation, the family thinking together. Dad talks about medicine,
science, his childhood in Australia, his forebears, selected stories about
the War, how he met Mum.
Mum talks about their wartime romance, England, history and family,
her vicarage childhood, Oxford; not much about the War because she
lost her brother in it, too painful to remember.

She once climbed into an attic and put out
an incendiary bomb with a bucket of sand.
Dad says she's plucky – a wartime word.
From my parents I understand that history asks you
to find out where you've come from,
the ancestral characters who compose your strand
that weaves through time.

~

I go inside familiar houses in my mind,
as I did the Flounder Inn when it was lost;
the copper in the wash-house at No 5
with a brick box on top where Dad steamed
cut-down wooden skis, bent the ends up,
coated them with boiling red ski-glisse
and screwed on metal edges, as clear as
the garden at No 23, on the swinging seat with Mum,
pouring a cup of Lapsang Souchong from a silver teapot,
eating Chocolate Sultana Pasties.

~

In my room
on a low pink chair
I sit to read my new
Shakespeare.

1963

Finally my period. So this is it.
It seems unfair to have to cope with this sort of thing.

~

Dad teaches us to sail in a fourteen-foot X-class yacht called *If*, which
won the Sanders Cup in 1953, a graceful clinker-built kauri craft, heavy,
without buoyancy tanks, with canvas sails, gaff-rigged, a bowsprit, a
steel centreboard which I have to haul up and down as we cross the
shallow places in Otago Harbour.

Dad commands in his naval voice
'Ready about! Lee – oh!'
The boom swings over, we duck,
she threatens to capsize.

The centreboard is too heavy for me
to operate reliably; just like the nutcracker
it comes off the pivot, falls down
causing chaos. On the trapeze,
hooked into a canvas belt
swinging out over the water, my small weight
balances the boat as it skims the waves.
Malcolm, Robert and I are crew, Dad a curt skipper.

~

From church I gain awareness of metaphor.
Prayer seems like a branch of poetry.
Confirmed at St Paul's Cathedral,
I express the desire to be a nun.
Mum thinks I might perhaps take after
Great Aunt Blanche, the deaconess.

~

I put aside the thought of being a nun
at Bible class camp on St Martin's Island.
A boy kisses me – in the wind
the tussock ripples like golden velvet.
I put my arms inside his jacket –
a shock, to feel his heart beat.

~

For the church social I make my first dress to a Simplicity pattern, in
crisp dark blue poplin with red roses, cut out on the dining-room floor
and sewn on the Singer.

Worn with a stiff petticoat it has a full skirt, darts in the bodice, two pockets. To make the ties at the back I sew the edges of long strips together then turn them inside out, using a wooden spoon.

Blue dress, red shoes, standing with my friends
on the girls' side of the hall. Boys watch
from the other side, come across and take us away
one by one. It's nerve-wracking, waiting to be chosen.

Dad's outside in the car at the time arranged, which is just before the last dance, so I miss the Destiny Waltz. He's stern. Ten minutes late. At home, Mum's in her dressing gown, hairpins in her hair, worrying; her worry worse than anger.

~

About a Singer

Tough bounciness of that wee tyre,
the silver lever pressing on the wheel,

The bobbin busy as a fishing reel
propelled by treadle or by nudging knee,

The wooden case, gold lettering, a tricky lock,
insistent pull of thread through metal

Apertures, the loop and clasp, whirr and attack
like an accelerating train, the stitches in a perfect line

Or else a tangle underneath. The fiddly tension.
The everlasting light in her black bonnet.

~

One morning in the kitchen
making toast for breakfast
we hear on the Bell radio which sits
on the shelf beside the yellow venetian blind
above the sink, a news flash:
the assassination of President Kennedy.
There's anguish in the reporter's voice.

~

Taking the miracle for granted now, I find my glasses an impediment.
Boys don't make passes – I want to find out what it means – go without
wearing them to *South Pacific* at the St James with a boy from Boys'
High.
We sit in the back row where the couples struggle quietly in the dark.
The screen is a big blur but I'm trying to follow the story when he puts
his arm over my shoulders and tries to kiss me, sideways.

~

Access to knowledge is via important tomes, *The Encyclopaedia
Britannica*, the Oxford dictionaries in the school library consulted
with reverence. At home, Mum and Dad are our resources: Mum
for anything to do with spelling, language, art and history; Dad for
medicine, maths, science. Malcolm became a physicist, Alison a potter
and artist, Fiona a professor of rheumatology, while I was subject to the
antigravity effect of poetry.

~

English, French, Latin, maths, history, general science, including
physics, popular because the young teacher is male, a rare occurrence,
and he has a Beatle haircut.

I appreciate, as if it were a poem,
the elegant Law of Moments.

~

1964

Reading all the time, at school, at home, in bed,
reading walking home from school along Highgate
so engrossed in Janet Frame I bump into a lamp-post.

At the library Mum and I walk along the shelves, our arms full of books.
One more, she says. She reaches up to *The Forsyte Saga* and puts it on
top of my pile. See how the family endures, its generations linked like
vertebrae, genetic cord inside.

Her own tree bears apples of history –
that erudite Doctor Fell of Oxford whom Tom Brown did not like;
Granville Sharp, working for the abolition of slavery;
the Bishop of St Asaph in the Tower;
Thomasina Grenville, widow of Sir Roger – was she watching
when he went down with the *Mary Rose*.

~

Dad's roots go back to the Western Isles. This St Kildan
eats his porridge standing up, thirsts for Wakatipu's oxygen
after the air-conditioning of the hospital where he works so hard
and comes home late; we're prowling around the kitchen
annoying Mum, who won't serve dinner without him.

The roll-topped desk in his study is rationally used;
papers in place, mail filed in drawers,
a blotter on the writing surface, the gold-nibbed
fountain pen no one's allowed to borrow,
with which he writes his medical lectures in rapid angular script
of even slope, intellectual control and energy, in black Quink.
Mum writes in Radiant Blue.
Dad's hand reminds me of Bartók; Mum's, Mozart.

He comes out of his study at eight o'clock for a cup of tea with Mum
in front of the Conray heater. On the tray a silver teapot, milk jug, two
teaspoons, sugar bowl, two cups and saucers, four biscuits, two plain,
two chocolate. It's their discussion time.

~

I blush at peer scrutiny, entering the morning classroom,
conscious of the gap between my teeth,
my ordinary hair, ordinary glasses.
I'm saving up for contact lenses.
Invited to a party, I spend hours in preparation.
At the last minute, applying eyeliner, spill
the brown-black contents of the bottle
down the front of my new double-buttoned
turquoise linen dress with white top-stitched lapels.

Rouge is fast; light lipstick, pink not red.
During the War, she says, some women drew seams
in eyebrow-pencil down the backs of their legs
to suggest silk stockings. The smooth suspender-clasp.
I gather there is some unstoppable force in men
that might be unleashed if you go too far.
Too far how?

~

Buddy Holly appeals to me,
sweet-voiced, that little hiccup, self-effacing
like the Shadows, especially Hank Marvin
with dark-framed glasses and stovepipe trousers.
Limpid eyes of Paul McCartney.

~

You need a proper twist dress to dance the peppermint twist.
A twist dress skims the waist, is hemmed with deep pleats or a frill

that swirls. You dance with a smooth sawing motion, elbows tucked in,
varying angles, swivelling your feet.

~

Scalloped curtains like fairytale ballgowns,
changing colour through the spectrum
during the music of the introduction before
'God Save The Queen', when everybody stands up.
Later, as rebellious students, we stay seated.

Each Dunedin cinema has character;
the St James a twinkling night sky ceiling,
the Century graceful Art Nouveau,
the ornate Regent, plush His Majesty's,
the State, the Embassy, the Octagon
beside the DIC with fashion models
behind plate-glass windows, a modern escalator,
the record shop where we buy jazz LPs
and 45s of the Top Twenty
that stack on the turntable of our record player.

~

Malcolm and I discover jazz. We listen to Oscar Peterson, Joe Pass,
Charlie Byrd, Milt Jackson, Django Reinhardt, Wynton Marsalis
for their lithe playing, ideas that dart, divert, disrupt, adapt, dance back
into a common stream of musical consciousness –
just writing their names brings their sound to my ear –
Wes Montgomery's guitar the best of all, full colour spectrum,
mind control.

~

Sun streams in the window of the sixth-form classroom.
Drowsy pleasure in the language of poetry
our English teacher reads to us – Keats, Shelley, Shakespeare,
Yeats, Hopkins, Dylan Thomas.

~

I develop skill in note-taking, fast and accurate handwriting.
History is examined in essay form, a pleasure.
Reading Virginia Woolf in English class
I recognise this stream of consciousness
from *Faces in the Water* and *The Edge of the Alphabet*,
placed in the Columba library by an astute librarian;
find more treasure there in Katherine Mansfield.
Dump maths, add German.
A Shakespeare prize subscribes me to the Athanaeum Library.
I discover Marilyn Duckworth's *A Gap in the Spectrum*,
which incites me to tint my hair red.

~

Miss Buchan, our small but terrifying
red-haired headmistress, rules us with indignation.
We're critical of her dress sense.
I can dance without pain in modern dance with Shona Dunlop
if I avoid arabesques.
In the school hall Mr Robinson, or Greasy Jack because of the
Brylcreem, and his small neat wife in a wide-skirted dress and high
heels, demonstrate the essential ballroom dances.

~

Mary Quant: nice name for the streamlined physics
of my black and white plastic hoop earrings,
mini-skirt, boots, new glasses with black frames,
a white flash at the upswept corners.

Ali, who irons her long hair draped over the ironing board
in a golden waterfall, resembles Twiggy,
requires Courrèges white boots.
We paint our black boots with white tennis shoe paint
but the paint cracks, black.

We're not supposed to lie around chatting
about the hit parade, homework, clothes and boys
on the phone in the hall. Our number is 73 202.

Ali shows me how to do the Mashed Potato.
You move your clasped hands around
as if rhythmically mashing potatoes,
circling the hips, stepping from foot to foot,
eyes half-closed, lips pouted,
a serene expression of inner concentration.

Malcolm's friend Robert Purves shares
our sense of humour. On his birthday we make
a giant cardboard and crêpe-paper cake,
take it to the front door of his house, ring the doorbell
and I pop out dressed as a fairy,
which seems to all of us extremely funny.

~

The kilt rolled over and hitched up, regulation green bloomers replaced,
if you can get away with it, by thigh-clinging witches' britches, red or
green, edged with lace. When our young English teacher marries,
we giggle uncontrollably
at a love-bite on her neck.
The other place for giggling is in church.

A group of us bike to school along Highgate.
On the way home we take off our hats,
let our hair out, buy a milkshake at the Roslyn Dairy.

One day there's a teddy boy in there
wearing winklepickers and lime green socks
he winks at me   I seem to float ...

~

Patient while I kangaroo and graunch, Dad teaches me to drive. Without too much shouting I obtain my driver's licence. Sometimes I borrow Mum's Hillman Imp and go for a drive to Port Chalmers, St Kilda beach, or up Signal Hill to the lookout above the city, where the heavy sculptures of the Early Settlers gaze glumly east and west.

~

Contact lenses at last, a fiddly business
but worth it to feel the air on my eyelids,
wear eyeshadow, eyeliner like Natalie Wood
in *West Side Story*. With a fine brush,
paint the line from the inner corner steadily across the top lid
to the outer corner, extending it with an upwards flick.

Seventeen magazine brings fashion to aspire to –
angel tops, chisel-toed shoes, a strap across the instep,
patent leather, black and white houndstooth mini-skirt,
patterned stockings, miraculous pantyhose.
The age of seventeen is miles away.
We iron our fringes, stick our kiss-curls to our cheeks
with Sellotape at night so they stay flat.

~

Apricots glow in the cool packing shed
where I pack Moorpark and Roxburgh Red
in a white pine box in rhythmic patterns.
My Christmas holiday job, fruit-picking in Clyde.
Boston buns iced pink and sprinkled
with coconut for morning tea, in the heat
of the dry rocky slopes above the Kawarau
chiselling its green chasm.

I enjoy my independence, experience
vomiting from too much cider.

1965

To improve our deportment we walk smoothly around
balancing books on our heads.
At my bedroom desk I'm reading, essay writing, working for
Scholarship exams, doing my best with Grace and Good Discipline
according to the motto on my hat badge.

~

Dress up for Friday night in town, venture
to the downstairs coffee bar in the Exchange,
the Hob Nob, below the Sanitarium shop
on Princes Street, for coffee and a cheese roll.
Among the leather jackets and bouffant hairdos,
listen to the jukebox.

~

When Marilyn Parker comes over we pretend we're swotting
for exams in my room but listen instead to the LP of Richard Burton
reading the love poems of John Donne, his resonant, sensual voice
teasing out word patterns to the limit of my understanding.

In history I learn a new word: Iconoclasm.

The word 'myrrh' doesn't sound as aromatic
as it looks, phonetically.

~

Stagestruck, in drama lessons at the Globe Theatre
with Rosalie Carey, intoning 'Ode to the West Wind'
I learn to project my voice,
learn poems and Shakespearean speeches, hope
for a walk-on part in one of Patric's productions
in the theatre adjoining their house.

In Friday night drama class Patric talks about world theatre,
especially the plays under production, whether Ibsen, Chekhov,
Albee, Ionesco, Aristophanes. He sits in the auditorium
two or three rows back and speaks to us, disposed on the stage
under the lights. His voice comes out of semi-darkness.
Our attention is intensified by self-awareness.
If we keep still, relaxing into the shape
our body makes, we can remain
listening intently for long periods.

Accents, intonation, movement, building characters
from within, mindful of Stanislavsky. After class we go –
Marilyn, Maureen, Gabrielle, Judy, Bill – for coffee
at the Sirocco Coffee Lounge in Dowling Street
crowding into the booth at the back, continuing
with the avant-garde till late
last trolleybus home
night lights
Gerry Mulligan
slick black Rattray Street
neon in the rain
The Dragon Café, the Diamond Grill.

~

A role at last, as Mae Rose Cottage in *Under Milk Wood*.
In the dressing room the adult actors transform themselves.
The scent of greasepaint gives me tingling stage fright;
I have a single line in the hot spotlight:
'I'll sin till I blow up.'

Dylan Thomas and Gerard Manley Hopkins
speak to my inner ear with lyric and sprung lines,
linguistic energy like Shakespeare's
and something else – their own dear selves as poets
who have sat down to write with pen and paper.

~

Grey gusts sweep the lake towards the beach at Frankton,
where Robert's parents have their holiday house.
Too rough for Robert to visit us today
in his white dinghy, *Cwmfyshrdlu.*
Often we see his wake
arrowing over glassy water,
hear the Seagull engine's chigchigchigchigchig.

Mercurial, the lake reflects the weather
fine-etched wind-fans flick the silver water
waves claw or kiss the shingle beach
The sky darkens
the lake darkens.

Out of the dark
eels rise to the light
of a fire on the beach,
waver in shallows
shadows on shingle.

~

Malcolm, Robert and I
flat on our backs on the hillside
stargazing
seeing how far we can think
Out There.

~

In the Scholarship English exam held in Marama Hall
I choose the essay topic 'A letter to my grand-daughter',
project my mind into the future, imagining
a grand-daughter named Alice and myself as a writer
looking back, giving her advice about life

as she herself begins to write. Now I do happen
to have a grand-daughter named Alice,
as well as Holly and Jack; though I had no ambition then
to be a poet, I've become one.

~

Away with my green jersey, prefect's badge,
my kilt, green hat, hat badge. I leave school
elated, with awards; Shakespeare bust, Dux.

I'd rather be going with Mum to England at Christmas
to visit Granny, but settle for a fruit-picking holiday
in Nelson before starting university.

Independent at last, my friend and I
immediately buy Capstan cigarettes and look out for boys,
hitchhike blithely, accept invitations to drink beer,
pick raspberries and apples to earn money.

A young woman worker shows me scars on her legs –
cigarette-burns from family abuse, she tells me.
I'm shocked, have an inkling of my ignorance.

On New Year's Eve we get a lift from the berry farm
to Motueka where we meet two hitchhikers
in boots and shorts, sitting on a stone wall by the church.
We all end up in Nelson at midnight drinking
Captain Morgan rum, the street knee-deep in broken bottles

Separated from my girlfriend
I go with tall, brown-bearded Ross
to his tobacco picker's hut:
surrender at dawn.
We fall in love, both for the first time.

I'm nearly seventeen, he's not much older,
a woodcarver from Auckland,
idealistic, intelligent, restless.

1966

As we walk back from Riwaka on New Year's Day,
defiantly I'm singing my favourite aria
from *Lucia di Lammermoor*,
of which Mum and I, liking the tragic romance,
had recently followed the score together at home.
'*Verranno a te sull'aure ...*' I sing this bright morning,
skipping down the dusty road
beside the loping legs of Ross.
We pause on a bridge to talk our hearts out
over a chuckling river.

~

I trace the spider-line I've left behind
through times I've lived,
anchored at particular points,
aware of the delicate nature of this operation,
remembering my place in the past.

Outlines, memory glossed in words –
it was and it wasn't like this, the grain is finer,
close-up grain of skin, hair, iris, breath,
details of wonder.

~

He hitchhikes north to see his mum. I come home to start the first term
at Otago.

In this energetic world of new ideas, friends, lecturers, lectures, constant
reading in English, French, German, philosophy, my attention is often
distracted by love letters from Auckland.
This annoys my mum.

~

A Lissie Rathbone Scholarship, enough to buy textbooks, bus fares,
lunch and coffee in the student union caf, sustenance for earnest
conversations about literature, art, politics.

Audrey Hepburn smokes with chic.
Raised in brand loyalty to Rinso, Colgate,
Ipana, Ajax, we automatically adopt personal
brands of cigarettes: Rothmans, Peter Stuyvesant,
Benson and Hedges, Rembrandt, Pall Mall,
Capstan, black Sobranie, coloured cocktail Sobranie,
Camel, the expensive oval Turkish ones
in a softly opening white box,
our chatter facilitated by the constant
offering and sharing of cigarettes
which prolongs the conversation
another five minutes and another five
until I've missed a lecture, oh dear,
might as well stay and talk another hour.

~

I find *Waiting for Godot*
a parable of great simplicity.

Theatre passion and my language studies
dovetail; Beckett in English and French,
Genet's inverted hierarchy, Cocteau beyond the veil,
Sartre's existentialism, Camus' benign, indifferent universe.
Ionesco's array of possible meanings
beyond the world's apparent surface

makes me wonder, how dependable is language
and all it carries of the world?

Adjust to this best of all possible worlds
even to the possibility of stepping
out of meaning altogether.

~

Nobody pays university fees.
We are given a fantastic education
by Aotearoa New Zealand.
We develop an independent manner of thinking.

~

A privileged child, I accept all this, along with my Columba education,
paid for by Mum from her teaching salary, join in with my peer group's
derision of bourgeois aspirations. Politically ignorant, I opt for the
power of art, avant-garde, rebellious thinking – not that there's much to
rebel against – my only avenue for rebellion
the more conventional life-path that might have been mine
had I not resisted attempts to steer me towards suitable young men.
My rebellion, of sorts, happened in the 1980s
in favour of autonomy and creative freedom.

~

Mum is all for women's liberation, social and intellectual, not sexual.
She and Dad are unhappy, forethinking ill, when Ross arrives in
Dunedin, finds a flat in London Street and sets up a woodcarving studio
in the front room.

On the way to my early morning lecture
in German, less fun than French,
I drop in for coffee; we end up in bed.

~

I wear a beatnik-style black sloppy joe, pale lipstick,
a rope of beads, mini-skirts, black tights, boots.
Stretch bell-bottomed jeans, green suede shoes,
an Emma Peel top with high neck and cutaway shoulders,
my shoulder-length auburn hair flipped up at the ends.

~

Ross finds a job at L.N. Martin's antique shop in George Street, carving
acanthus scrolls and linenfold panels, repairing antique furniture,
making three-legged stools, pairs of bellows, carved sea-chests.
Pipe in his mouth, bearded, in a dark blue seaman's jersey, with fierce
attention sharpening his chisels, he makes just enough to pay the rent.
I learn the woods – Pākehā woods, oak, mahogany, oregon – marvel at
shining chisel cuts, spend ages sanding finished swirls for chair backs
and chiffoniers, to speed things up, because the rent is always behind.

Tilt of his head, glinting blade,
hair on lean forearms
caught in sunlight
at the work-bench by the window
in London Street.

~

The University Dramatic Society holds auditions for Aristophanes'
Lysistrata in Allen Hall. Rodney Kennedy casts me in the title role.
Stricken by childhood polio so that his legs are short but his head man-
sized, he's outrageously sharp-tongued and funny. In rehearsals as he
chain-smokes, some ash and perhaps a potato chip or a pea left over
from lunch lie on his glasses, around his neck on a cord.

~

I'd like to go flatting but Mum and Dad say no,
there's a perfectly good bedroom at home.
I renovate it; dye the chenille bedspread orange,
paint a mural eight feet long, red and gold sunburst

ribbons of light. Pin up a Tom Field woodcut,
a poster of Che Guevara.

After seeing plays by Chekhov, Shaw, Lorca
I rush to the library to read their works.
My serious interest in drama leads me into
Brecht, Artaud, Jarry; to Magritte, Miro;
film festivals – genius of Marcel Marceau
in *Les Enfants du Paradis*; Fellini's *8 1/2*;
Buñuel's *The Discreet Charm of the Bourgeoisie.*

~

Patric's a bearded presence with long hair,
dark-framed glasses and a memory able to quote
in conversation anything from Aeschylus
to Yevtuschenko. I never can quote with confidence
for fear of error.

The Globe itself is a stage set of flimsy construction,
draped with brocade curtains, shadowy, elegant.
In the auditorium a bucket intercepts
a melancholy drip from the roof. There's an exhibition
of McCahon's waterfall paintings in the foyer.
I feel the undercurrents between the adult actors,
glimpse their intersecting lives.

~

In the Green Room at Allen Hall, into an echoing oubliette
between stone walls, empty beer bottles drop with a glassy crash.
Beside the window, the chaise longue where many students kiss.
Relationships arise among the cast, endure or fade
when the season's over.
There's always time for rehearsing, at night or between lectures.
In the dressing room before the bright mirror, with greasepaint,
costume and inward concentration, we become our characters.

Once I drank too much red wine before going on stage – only once –
except that time at the Robbie Burns
when Hone plied me with spirits until it was too late
and I had to chair a literary discussion, which was okay
until my voice swooped, my poise collapsed,
I really can't remember.
Hone chuckled – 'Teach you a lesson, see?'

1967

In *Little Brother, Little Sister*
Jim Wright and I act in complete accord.
It's a sweet love story. Sometimes we're cast
in radio plays recorded at the New Zealand Broadcasting Corporation
studios in Albany Street, learning the nuanced art of radio.
Jim gives a performance in *Marat/Sade* as the Herald, which suits his
form and grace.

Ian Ralston from the NZBC comes to our drama class
to tape our voices with multi-layering and echo
on a reel-to-reel tape recorder for a production
of *The Bacchae*.
I see the recording process. I hear my voice,
which has come from inside me, from the outside.
It's startling, like seeing myself from another point of view.

~

Syntax, precision instrument of meaning,
dictée, grammar, vocabulary, translation.
I envisage a job as an interpreter,
memorise Baudelaire, Apollinaire, Verlaine,

Rimbaud, study the scansion of French poetry,
rejoice in the alexandrine, discover Prévert.

~

Ross and I cool off,
mix with a wider group of friends.
Mum's pleased – I find it liberating –
reading Simone de Beauvoir's *The Second Sex*
I recognise that I'm a woman
amid a surrounding presence of women's
sharp sight and care.

~

In rehearsal for *The Balcony*
I'm summoned to be fitted for a costume
at Rodney's house in Alva Street.
James Mack has a cardboard box of ostrich feathers
and lacy things set out on the table
near a window seat looking over the harbour
at the other end of the room from a painting by McCahon
of the sinuous green Otago Peninsula.
In this dress-up box are stockings, lace, ribbons,
feather boas, corsets, hats and gloves.
Laughing at Rodney's naughty jokes,
James creates a sparkly black tiara
with ostrich feathers standing up behind the peak.
In the brothel, The Balcony, I am to wear
a strapless black lace corset and fishnet stockings.
I like this risqué costume.

Lyndon Cowell has designed the set
with a gauze cyclorama, creating art nouveau
layers of reality. The fantasies play out within the rooms
while outside, real-life insurrection rages.

Paul Richardson plays my client, the General.
We act out his fantasy.
Live acoustic space,
voice-music foldback.
In our poetic, erotic scene
of the General and his Horse on the battlefield,
war's fatal beauty whips up erotic
tension in the audience –
I whinny and prance,
I kiss his sword,
unaware of the impression made
by my performance on members
of the English Department
seated in the front row.

~

Taking to the idea of alienation
I dive into Camus, Sartre, Kafka,
go alone to an afternoon session of *The Trial*
in the State Theatre, exit into a grey
rainy night in George Street.
Sometimes Dunedin looks extremely dull.

~

The Byrds, Donovan, Dylan, as much Beat poetry
as I can find in the University Bookshop.
Leftish, idealistic, politically uninformed,
I see Tim Shadbolt from afar
speaking of the Vietnam war,
see *Doctor Strangelove*
and a frightening film about nuclear disaster,
learn of radioactivity, nuclear testing,
the abominably long half-life of fallout.
Escape into *Antigone*.

In short, I live in a happy, ignorant, opinionated
undergraduate bubble.

~

Students ambush James K. Baxter in the caf
where tables strewn with cups, plates, papers,
straws, ashtrays, orange peel are pushed together
to accommodate monster discussions, students
missing lectures to join his company
over black coffee and the thin brown
cheroots he smokes.

I'm truly stricken with hero worship
when I knock on the door of the Burns Fellow's study.
'What poetry shall I read?' He says, 'Fleur Adcock,
Anything but Curnow.'
He gives me a newly written poem, 'Summer 1967'.
This poem is of the world I know.
I learn it by heart.

I admire him with an enthusiasm that leads to my
embracing him, deeply impressed as I am
by his poetry reading on the stage of the Globe
one rainy Sunday afternoon,
where he resembles his portrait by Els Noordhof,
hunched in a raincoat against imagined storms.
The voice of oiled, metallic timbre.

He gave me a statuette of the Virgin Mary and a silver medal of the
same, of intricate detail, which I always kept close by until the time I
drove away from the Flounder Inn, never seeing it again.

~

We girls live at home, Ali and Fio growing into their own attractive
looks and independent lives. Malcolm's flatting in a house on the corner

of Union Street referred to as 'Peasmouldia'. Studying astrophysics,
he's building a radio telescope at Invermay to intercept the background
radiation of the universe.

~

We spend family holidays at Frankton
while the houses spread and jet-boats multiply
snarling in to the beach below us.
In Queenstown we laugh at tourists
gawping from buses at the landscape.

~

At the end of the year Mum arranges a trip for me to New Caledonia, to
stay with a French family, to improve my oral French. I'm taken to visit
the family's nickel mine.
In a red earth bowl men are digging, loading the dust onto a clanking
conveyor belt leading to a ship, this cargo to be taken offshore and
minted into nickel money and brought back as the light Pacific currency
in which their wages are paid.
Terra nullius again, perhaps.
A crack in my complacency,
now I'm aware of the Pacific and its people.

1968

J.K. Baxter and Patric, clad much the same
in homespun jerseys, deeply conversing
in the kitchen behind the theatre.
As I flit past them in my costume
for *Mr O'Dwyer's Dancing Party*
they hail me as Penthesilea.

A line from *The Bureaucrat* stays in my mind:
'Politeness killed her.'

~

Kids on the Road

kids on the road
I am that one trailing sideways
in the pink dress
interested in stones
you know, I would like to kick
t.s. eliot in the head
because you shouldn't have to pass
english exams to love poetry
I don't want any more maps
a silk thread would be better
where I am going now is
stopping for shivers
woggly trees in puddles
might be a coin on the road
a rusty key
no more puzzles for clever sleuths
I'd just like to
smile at you broadly
and hand you the whole world
clean on a plate.

~

A creative group of friends
inhabit the flat above the North End Wineshop
on the corner of Howe and Great King.
Front door on Howe Street. You enter below
and go upstairs to the landing, turn right into the lounge,
a couple of bedrooms through there, straight ahead
to the kitchen, cups and mugs containing mould,

or left into Ross's studio, a long room above the street
where he carves when he's not reading Dostoyevsky.
He makes wooden bowls, salad servers,
carved sea-chests, leather sandals, three-legged stools.
From a kauri verandah post he carves
the graceful golden head of a gazelle.
He's broke – has to sell it
to Charlton Edgar at the Art Gallery.

We listen to the lyrics of the Byrds, Donovan,
Peter, Paul and Mary (who once dropped in to a party
after their concert), play Bob Dylan continuously,
learn him by heart, talk about plays, films, books
art, drink wine if we can afford it. There's always music
and talk; young intellectual Bridie Lonie,
bright-eyed Marian Evans, Bill McKay painting
or learning lines for his role in *Eh!*,
Ross the woodcarver, Peter Olds the poet
playing chess with J.K. Baxter
to the bittersweet strains of Dylan.

Between and after lectures I spend hours there,
attracted by an intelligent vivacity
that frequently devolves into a party –
once, a log fell out of the fire as we danced
and the floor caught alight.
I'm usually home by midnight.

~

The Star Fountain, a watery maze of pipes
and arrangements of nozzles, takes up
most of the lower Octagon. At certain times
it leaps to life – Bavarian marches
or Strauss waltzes blare from speakers,
jets of water spout singly and in groups,

swirling under the spotlights, changing colour
in time with the music. After a few minutes
the jets and music reach a climax and subside.

Students roving around the Octagon
in the small hours, picking flowers for Robbie Burns
or climbing up to sit in his bronze lap,
like to add detergent to the water
or, prey to the fascination of the soft lead nozzles,
get into the fountain and bend them outwards
so they shoot in all directions,
drenching passers-by at the next performance.

~

J.K. Baxter hands out copies of a newly printed
broadsheet, 'A Small Ode on Mixed Flatting':
subversive, from behind a cloak of myth.
We all read *The Little Red Schoolbook*,
as banned and interesting as *Ulysses*.

~

Bill Mackay plays Feste in *Twelfth Night* at the Globe
with the air of a wry Pierrot. There's a satiny quality
to Marilyn Parker's voice savouring the language of Olivia.
I do front-of-house for several performances
for a free seat in the back row where I can follow the script.

I hope to go to drama school in Birmingham
when I've finished my degree at the end of the year.
Mum will arrange for me to board with Aunt Marnie
while I study to be a professional actress
at a school attached to the Birmingham Rep,
but it is not to be
because

Invited to a twenty-first birthday party
Ross and I go to Rodney's beforehand and drink
champagne cocktails: a sugar cube, brandy, champagne,
a dash of bitters. Rodney pours drinks and teases
handsome heterosexual Ross in his brown suede jacket,
sending us tipsily on our way.
I stay the night with Ross and shortly afterwards
find I'm going to have a baby.

~

So instead of being a feckless arts student
I have to face adult reality.
Like a kaleidoscope shifting,
the elements the same but differently arranged,
everything's changed.

There is a test. General shock.
General Post.
Bang goes drama school.
Shotgun marriage arranged.
I feel sorry but excited.

After a terse communication in the newspaper, at Labour weekend
in the Edinburgh House registry office,
I in a cream silk dress, Ross in a dark suit,
Mum in tears, Dad grim,
with two friends as witnesses, very briefly
we are married. Now I'm Mrs Smith.

~

Afterwards we go back to the flat in Cargill Street with a couple of
bottles of champagne, sitting on the floor, our belongings and books in
tea-chests.
A weekend at a motel on the St Clair waterfront – it's chilly. We feel a bit
dull after all the fuss. I miss my family. On the first morning I feel sick at

the smell of frying bacon.
La Nausée, I'm pregnant, I've left home.

~

Ross has found some carving work.
For a student holiday job at Cherry Farm
I need a reference, ask J.K. Baxter to write one for me.

He gives me two: one conventional, for the job,
the other affectionately bawdy. He says by way
of explanation that the academics are a funny lot –
there'd been lively discussion at morning tea
of my role as the General's Horse in *The Balcony*.

One day J.K. Baxter comes to the door of our flat
collecting for the Salvation Army. I wail
that I only have one dollar. He looks at me hard,
takes it and puts it in his tin. Both he and Hone
taught me lessons about material possessions.

J.K. Baxter kept in touch when he went to Jerusalem,
from where he wrote to me in New Plymouth,
ending one letter, 'There are many people
to love here, but you are always in my heart.'

1969

How young Ross and I were. I was in love with him again. He was
ambivalent. He felt caught in this shotgun marriage. I felt caught out by
my woman's body, which until then I hadn't really believed, somehow. It
being the sixties, there was a scandal,
hard on Mum and Dad.

A newspaper clipping arrives from his mother
with an ad for a woodcarver in New Plymouth.
We're off to New Plymouth for a woodcarving job.
We rent a house near Ngamotu beach.

On my back in the sun on the grass,
my stomach sticks up like a small hill.
Lying there, I feel an earthquake.
A jolt under my shoulderblades, a very deep noise.
My baby kicks.

~

Ross's job falls through. A rent problem. Intermittently he finds work
seagulling at the wharf but there's no money. A lean diet for pregnancy,
I'm always hungry. I remember the sirloin of beef that we won at a fair
on the Wheel of Chance, the kindness of Averill Brandon and her son
Nick, skilful potter.
I find a part-time job teaching English at a convent, my first teaching
experience. I like the nuns. I copy Mum. It's fun – teaching *Macbeth* –
meanwhile graduate *in absentia* with a senior arts prize from Otago.

~

Ross sketches a woodcut of me one morning
walking up the hill to catch the bus holding an umbrella
wearing my brown corduroy dress and long boots.

I cry when I lose my wallet on the bus
with my sorely needed pay packet in it.

~

For the baby's things we have a cupboard
painted white with orange and yellow flowers,
a white cane bassinette for which I sew a yellow
gingham frill, a wooden rocking chair
where I can nurse the baby.

Ross saw this rocking chair in the window
of a second-hand shop, liked the musical curves
of its dark wood, spoke-shaved spindles
of the back, the curved, adzed seat,
rockers worn with age.
It wasn't expensive but we had to scrape
our bank book out to buy it. The chair
bore a hand-written ticket
attesting that it had been made by the hand
of a whaler, of New Plymouth.

An elderly Māori woman comes to the door.
'May I have some of your flax
to make a kete?' I laugh, 'It's not my flax.'
She looks beyond me to the chair.
'What a beautiful chair to rock the baby in,
you are very lucky.' The next day she comes again
with a newly woven basket. In it is a piece
of pure white linen and a five cent piece,
for an ice-cream for the baby.
When I remember the chair, my memory of this woman follows.
She gazes past my shoulder.

~

At John Maynard's house
there's a room with paintings
hung around four walls
like windows
black as my Black Beauty.

~

July 11. Baby arrives!!!
An alert person
of lucent intelligence
my fair-haired daughter

awake to the world
at once
I hold her to my heart.

~

July 20, black and white TV,
Neil Armstrong walks on the moon.

~

It seems that work will always be a problem. We move to Auckland, find
a flat in Newmarket but the jobs don't last, the money situation's worse,
there are fleas in the carpet. We haven't heard of an unemployment
benefit. But we have friends, we live like students – I can see the good
side – I'm quite bohemian in outlook
but there's barely money to buy food.
I spend a lot of time in the Domain with my wee girl in her pushchair,
browse the bookshops, miss my academic work.
Not a hippie at heart, I feel we're drifting.

~

My daughter's birth naturalised me, for which I'm grateful.
By her arrival I was prevented from returning to England
and possible reversion to the northern hemisphere.
It's not unusual to have a baby in tow,
considering the hazards of contraception.
In San Francisco, later, I was introduced
to Carl Djerassi, inventor of the contraceptive pill.
In his art-filled apartment I saw my first Kandinsky –
shape and colour – perfect pitch ...

~

Tired of hippiedom, for once I make a practical decision – to go back to
Dunedin and improve my degree, then support us by teaching.

1970

21 Montgomery Avenue is near the university
beside the Leith, which has a peaceful, flowing sound
except when it floods to within inches of its banks.
When Ross launched a kayak into the Leith in flood
he nearly drowned as it whisked him downstream, breaking up his
craft, of which all he found later was a paddle.

We have flatmates, a cosy kitchen. Woodchips.
In my navy blue jersey and jeans
I'm a student again. I've chosen to do Honours in early twentieth-
century modern French literature and the notion of the Absurd. There's
plenty of reading. Ray Stone, Roger Collins, Elizabeth Goulding, Roy
Dineen and Nola Leov are my lecturers.

~

I hear that my friend Marion McLeod has been swept away
by a serious young poet with long fair hair.

~

At Allen Hall Rodney casts me in Olwen Wymark's
thoughtful, poetic *The Inhabitants*.

~

In Andrea's bedroom we're reading *The Lion in the Meadow*.
I brush her long fair hair, silk in my hands. Andrea knows the words of
her storybooks by heart, insists that they be read with accuracy. She has
an advanced vocabulary. When I'm at lectures she meets her best friend
Syneve at the university crèche, a new establishment blessed by the
student mothers.

~

Ross can't settle.
I dive deeper into reading, lectures, essays.
In the end he hitchhikes away, meets somebody else, stays away.

The first entries in my journal are about a horrible feeling of alienation.

I write for company and to sort out my emotions, dismayed at the turn
my life has taken. With the help of my family and my studies I contain
the shock; reading Villon,
hoist myself out of the difficult present through the long-ago
consciousness of a poet.

I have to find a teaching job.
Resilience, says Dad, is a gift you have; use it.
Slowly heartbroken but happy with Andrea,
I complete the academic year.

~

At the end of the year there's a Christmas party at Robert May's place.
A Māori artist, the 1969 Frances Hodgkins Fellow, has brought mussels
and cockles from the beach at Aramoana. We talk in the kitchen where
he's preparing them with garlic, wine and butter. He's lived in Vence,
in the south of France, painting at the Karolyi Foundation. We talk all
evening about Dada, Surrealism, Picasso, Matisse, Miro 'taking a line for
a walk'. After the party he drives me home to Montgomery Avenue, says
goodbye. He's off up north for the holidays.

1971

A two-room flat on Highgate, close to Hart Street and Columba.
Andrea's settled at the crèche, I'm earning a living teaching (with advice
from Mum); my new uniform an academic gown. I teach English,
French and Latin, find it easier to teach three languages than one; we
move between them among the roots of words, compare grammar and
vocabulary, blur boundaries in digressions, games, plays, songs. I feel the
living circuit of the classroom, read my students in their handwriting.

~

Maud the A40 Somerset smells of leather seats and oil leaks.
A chrome grille like a pursed mouth
between sky-blue cheeks, a canvas baby chair
hooked over the front passenger seat, not safe
but she's built like a tank.
Parked outside school one day she was rear-ended
by a poor wee Anglia whose radiator disintegrated,
wrecked by Maud's staunch boot.
(Eventually I sold her to Hone Tuwhare for $50.)

~

A letter from the Māori artist up north.
Ralph's handwriting in my consciousness.

~

Andrea and I drive over the motorway in Maud
to visit Marian Evans, Bill Mackay and Dylan.
There's a spacious feeling, a bareness in Marian's house –
sunshine in her hair, ringing laughter
at Seacliff near the railway line – sea light,
scent of linseed oil, turps, paint,
Bill's many paintings of a tree,
fresh linen in a washing basket,
Andrea and Dylan playing on the swing,
long grass, clay scars of the slipping green coast, old fence posts,
marine breeze, blue sky, sun and shadow.

Peter Olds doesn't say much; friendly and shy in his black duffel coat,
poet with a notebook in his pocket,
he cautiously speaks his mind.
Juanita Ketchel might have stepped out of a pre-Raphaelite painting.
Long, tendrilled red-gold hair, pale aquiline features, a sweet, off-beat,
tentative way of speaking.

~

One night Ralph arrives at the Highgate flat in the dented green Land
Rover.
Black jersey, blue suede jacket, paint-spattered jeans,
dark hair, dark beard, wide smile. He's brought me a painting,
black lacquer buffed with lambswool to a reflective surface
which seems to contain soft moving shadows
that curl like smoke.
Down the centre of the panel sing three slim lines of yellow-gold and
orange.
He's thirty-nine, a worldly man to me at twenty-two – we fall in love
and then love deeply, explore the space between us,
talk for hours, touch, learn each other's minds.

~

121 Forth Street is a weatherboard cottage, painted red-brown with
white window frames, a white picket fence and a porch over the front
door, at the top of the Forth Street rise. The Land Rover's handbrake
failed; it just missed four parked cars
when it ran down the hill by itself one night,
nearly to Verkerk's Campus Wonderful Store.

A narrow hallway down the middle, a fireplace between the front room
and kitchen, two bedrooms, a cast-iron bedstead with brass knobs,
dark-painted wallpaper, framed paintings. Lean-to bathroom, toilet
downstairs. An ash tree between the kitchen window and the brick wall
of the house next door, gas stove in the corner of the kitchen, oval kauri
table near the window, Barningham cast-iron coal range with small
doors in the flue that can be opened and the lid removed to make an
open fire that's drawn back up the chimney.

Paintings and drawings everywhere, Ellis, Hanly, McCahon, Smither,
Harris.
Many female nudes drawn in ink and pencil. Nervy, telling lines.
(I'm abashed, at first.

He draws naked women.
I know some of them.)

~

In the shadowy hallway hang three paintings that seem completely
black.
When light slants in from the front door I see that the matt canvas
is textured with words in thicker paint, black on black, mysteriously
melding the words Malady, Melody, My Lady: Bill Manhire's poetry.
As the words change, meanings change and increase.
I hear the tonal quality of these black paintings telling the poem in a
repetitive, personal chant of poet and artist,
voices not raised above a murmur.

~

When Ralph brings friends home from the Captain Cook,
shellfish, fish, whitebait appear on the kitchen bench.
I dash for my French cookbook, a prize from school,
La Cuisine Familiale et Pratique.

We hear from a visitor about the Save Manapouri campaign
against the plans to raise Lake Manapouri, for electricity to power
an aluminium smelter at Tiwai Point.
This means drowning a pristine lake.
Reminds me of the nickel insult.

~

He goes every day to the new studio at 2 Aurora Terrace, Port Chalmers,
on the hill below Bully Hayes' flagpole. There are four small rooms
upstairs; downstairs a low-ceilinged kitchen. He's fixing up the kitchen
and ricketty steps down the narrow garden full of blackberry, sloping to
the harbour, islands and channel, the hills and Hereweka, the peninsula
across the water, different in all lights and weather.

Soup simmering on the coal range.
I've brought a loaf of bread. He pours red wine,
holds the glass up to the light.
Shades of red.
In harmony.

He needs more room to work, knocks out all the upstairs walls to make
an open space, leaving the brick chimney free-standing in the middle.
Leadlight windows across the front wall
divide the panorama into delicate frames.

He takes
a long time
working
in complete absorption.

I watch, hold my breath – a painting
made before my eyes –
he stops, stands back, wholly given
to looking,
steps in again.

~

A black goat called Sebastian
ate all the blackberry
and teatowels.

~

As Mum and I, so Andrea and I, our understanding
clear as an ice-cream scoop. We drive in Maud to Aramoana
to picnic with Anna and Syneve, pick blue-lipped mussels from the
rocks, run all over the beach, climb the high sandbank against the cliff
to run down leaping, flying. Spread out the tartan rug in the sandhills
out of the wind, unpack cups, milk, teaspoons, thermos, sandwiches of
home-made bread.

Anna's dark eyes shining, jade seagrass, skylarks, children's laughter.
Suddenly a seal!

~

Take a handful from the fleece,
tease it out gently,
keep your tension right.
He teaches me to spin.

I spin a whole long-stapled white fleece,
ply, wash, wind it, crochet peggy-squares
to make a double blanket for our bed.
It takes weeks of spinning every night, then crocheting
the spun, plied wool that varies in thickness
as I learn to keep it even. I like these imperfections,
knots and thinnesses,
times when the thread ran through my fingers
too fast or too slow.

I spin a dark brown fleece, knit him a Beat-fashion
sloppy joe. He cuts and sews a piece of hide to make
a leather hat with a plaited band. He smokes a pipe,
dark-haired and bearded, smile creasing his cheeks,
a fleet, intelligent gleam between us.
I love his modesty, soft voice, quick mind.

In his former life in Auckland he was married and divorced, he says,
and speaks no more about it. I understand that it was long ago.
He calls me wet behind the ears.
I feel like a licked-by-its-mother-tongue wobbly-balancing-four-square
newborn foal. I hope we might have a baby, but he says quietly,
it's unlikely.

~

Unfortunately there doesn't seem to be much money in art.
I am thankful for my teaching job.

~

Age of Aquarius – *Hair* comes to town. At Mo Knuckey's
we have lunch with the cast. Exciting energies
in their voices, colours, Afro hairdos, beads, kaftans, rhythm.

~

Le Malade Imaginaire, She Stoops to Conquer –
I love the playwrights for all the language they've instilled in me,
whole plays once known by heart, no longer subject to recall,
still living in my language store.

~

In the kitchen I'm marking a pile of exercise books while Ralph's at the
oval table,
of which the top slopes slightly, one of the legs of its pedestal askew due
to borer, drawing with pen and ink the cover for *Landfall 100*.
With quick, sure hand he paints an arch – looks up, grins,
Gateway or tombstone?

1972

Rosalie's agile enunciation
precisely placing teeth   lips   tongue
in sibilants   plosives   fricatives
with diaphragmatic breath
control air vibrating in the
sound-chamber of her mouth
renders the voice an instrument of music

She works hard at the Globe, housekeeping for an eccentric husband,
two young children and a white cat called Wibble-Wobble who walks
through performances at whim, whether Sophocles or Shakespeare.
She gives elocution lessons in and maintains the theatre,
amateur Dunedin actors rehearsing at all hours in her living room
or celebrating in her kitchen after the performance.

Saint's Day's long speeches train my memory. In Patric's rehearsals we
tease out Whiting's argument, work on the phrasing, make all clear. I
feel the vital energy flow between actor and audience, the quality of
attention.

~

At Forth Street Ralph puts in a stained-glass window
reclaimed from a derelict church out past Mosgiel somewhere,
builds steps of thick kauri planks leading downstairs under the ash tree.
We come home one day to find pinned to the door a note
from the building inspector, to the effect that we have no building
permit.
Action Will Be Taken.
I'm worried they might make him pull it all down.

But Ralph is opposed to building permits.
He has a word with somebody,
the way men do between themselves.

~

We hear that his mother,
Ana Maria, has passed away.
He and Hone Tuwhare go to her tangi at Mitimiti.
Hone writes a poem for her,
'A Fall of Rain at Mitimiti'.

~

I read *Pounamu, Pounamu,*
start a correspondence course in te reo Māori.
Ralph's working on a drawing series
incorporating proverbs referring to the land.
I learn the history of Parihaka, quiet
determination of Te Whiti, Tohu and the people,
see how whanau are interwoven.

~

Ralph designs a cover for *Islands I*, produces
drawings for Bill Manhire's *The Elaboration,*
Ted Middleton's *The Loners,*
Hone Tuwhare's *Sapwood and Milk.*
I watch him doing several portraits of Bill,
more like cryptic maps of the inside of a mind,
until he gets the clear, open lines he's looking for.

Ted comes over for a game of chess, a glass of red wine and earnest talk.
Ralph is concerned that Ted is going blind.
Ted gets up very close to Ralph's painting,
inspects it all over with intense concentration.
Ralph's portrait catches Ted in even fewer marks.

~

When red wine, swapped for a painting,
arrives in a barrel from Diana Balich, we have a bottling party,
dozens of glass flagons lined up all the way down the hall
and into the kitchen, everybody filling and corking.

~

Under the academic gown preserving me from chalk dust
I test the staff dress code with mini-skirts, culottes,
even a trouser suit, then move on to denim.
Chalk-skreeeek paroxysms. Hysteria when a wasp
enters the classroom – it's hard to continue teaching calmly.

Chalk dust, contact lenses – revert to glasses –
carbon paper, cranky copiers, Banda, Gestetner,
inky machinery, paper, time divided by buzzers and bells.

For my after-school dance class I choreograph a science-fiction ballet
to the trumpet of Don Ellis's 'Despair to Hope',
borrow from the Globe wardrobe some odd-shaped papier-mâché
silver helmets, created by James Mack for *Hamlet 2000*.

~

The potential of new surfaces, the timbre of expression they allow –
some sort of translation between languages – buffed lacquer reflects you,
polished swirls hover between inside and outside,
subtle shades of black absorb your gaze.

A postcard in the letterbox – a 'Pine' poem from Bill Manhire.
Enigmatic messages trigger a spate of drawing; Ralph writes and sprays
the words in paint, then goes on to print with the antique letters of a
wooden alphabet a whole series of 'Pine' and some funny 'Victoria'
prints, using old-fashioned stamps of soldiers on horseback, steam
trains and a nude woman, on the cast-iron Columbian hand press in the
Bibliography Room.

~

I'm shocked to hear of J.K. Baxter's death.
I mourn this light lost.

He saw the poet in me.
I am so sad I wasn't able to send him some white chocolate
as he asked in a letter from Jerusalem.
Now I can never make it up to him.

1973

'Requiem' for Antony Watson
and for Ana Maria.
Black, mauve, indigo, cello,
immaculate strings
on a shimmering surface
densely textured, layer on layer
of rain or tears

~

Charles Brasch, poet and editor of high, clear intellect, has died.
Somebody brings a copy of his poem written in hospital, 'Winter
Anemones', about the flowers brought to his bedside by Margaret Scott.

I met Charles only once, when he invited us to dinner to meet the
Aboriginal poet Oodgeroo Noonuccal, known as Kath Walker. The
atmosphere was courteous, the food perfectly prepared; I didn't take
part in the conversation, being over-awed by Charles and not knowing
much at all, it seemed, about literature. There was a side dish of
perfectly peeled white turnips.

~

The Polytechnic wants to acquire 121 Forth Street for its expansion.
Ralph is adamant: we will not sell. I am dismayed by official letterheads.
This situation carries on – there is a precedent – a house that made the
university library lose a corner.

~

Each month the World Record Club sends us classical music and jazz.
I have just put on Glenn Gould playing Bach when a sharp earthquake
rattles the house, the needle   jumps,
digs a short deep scratch.
This particular moment, this singular event, recorded.

~

With help from Dad we move to 27 Harbour Terrace, Careys Bay: a two-
storey white weatherboard house with a green roof, a verandah around
three sides edged with white iron lace, facing north to Aramoana.

We wake up to a light-filled landscape,
hardly believe our eyes and ears,
hop out of bed and breathe sea air,
have breakfast on the verandah
sitting on the old church pew, listen
to the birds, the train as it passes
the railway crossing above the back garden.

Space to move, unfolding wings, plenty of walls to hang the paintings on.
We paint the bedrooms – dark green for Andrea, dark red for us – sew
curtains and cushions on the Singer, arrange our new house with
delight, collect furniture – a dining table, Scotch chests, wardrobes,
antique chairs, a pale yellow silk lampshade with long bead tassels.

~

Ralph makes a maquette for a competition to design a mural for the
Hamilton Founders Theatre. The proposed wall area is wide and high;
he'll build this painting in panels to be attached to a framework behind,
fitted together with accuracy, not a join visible.

On a black ground, spectral colours unite an elegant abstraction
of confluent rivers, peoples, spiritual houses,
sacred enduring strength of whakapapa.

~

The Reverend Donald Phillipps conducts our wedding, a simple
ceremony at the studio in Aurora Terrace.
Maureen Hitchings has transformed the light-filled room
into a chapel, surrounding us with sculptures, paintings, candles,
flowers, vibrant panels and test-pieces for the mural.

The reception is a dinner party, catered by Rodney in his drawing room.
Dad provides the champagne.

Ralph has adopted Andrea in the Family Court. She and I change to
Hotere; again I give away my maiden name. Andrea adopts him too –
now he's her dad.

~

There's not enough room in the studio
but the old Love Construction Company building
on the foreshore below is empty.

There's plenty of space to stand the large panels against the walls,
spray them with undercoat, black lacquer in multiple layers,
lay them on trestles, cut and polish them.
Jet black. Veils and layers of black, reflective,
light-infused as the colours appear on the surface
in grades, progressions, strings.

It's time-consuming, meticulous work
with spray-gun, compressor and power tools.
He works long hours and comes home tired,
with headaches from the paint and thinners.

Sam Pillsbury comes with a crew to film him working on the mural.
Intently the cameras observe the artist scribing lines on pristine
surfaces,
mixing the colours
shade by subtle shade
in jam jars, with a stick.

In the Land Rover we all racket down
the bumpy road to Murdering Beach, so steep
the horizon seems to rise as we descend,
like a bowl filling up with water.

~

In Whiting's *The Devils* I become a nun, Sister Jeanne of the Angels,
Mother Superior of St Ursula's convent in Loudun. Huntly Eliott plays
the priest Grandier, Richelieu's critic, with whom Jeanne becomes
obsessed to the point of psychic possession. My role is vocally
demanding; Jeanne and her devils require a weird array of voices.

Ralph completes the set drawings for the play in one session, painting
words of the Latin Mass in watercolour swathes, a mediaeval feeling of
shadowy cloisters.
He and Patric build the set together. *The Devils* is the last production
by Patric at the Globe before he retires to live at Lake Mahinerangi,
completely giving up theatre. After all those plays, he says he is burnt
out. At the farewell party on the stage of the Globe, I drink champagne
and feel a sense of loss.

1974

We visit the Careys at Lake Mahinerangi.
Below the surface of this lake lies the drowned village,
Waipori. When the water level is high, it laps
at the front doorstep of the old farmhouse.
Skeletal trees jut black when the lake is low.
Mahinerangi can turn eerie pewter-grey sheeted with pale gold light.

It is lovely
to sit in a dinghy
on calm water
while Belinda and her friend play oboe and flute.

~

One afternoon Andrea and I come home to Careys Bay to find one
wall of the kitchen gone. Ralph has decided to enlarge it. He builds
with recycled timber a floor, ceiling, walls, puts in leadlight windows,
a skylight; we soak the planed boards with linseed oil; we sand and
polyurethane the floor, build shelves for all the pottery.
A refectory table made of thick golden kauri, an arched brick fireplace
for a coal range backed with salt-glazed bricks. Warm and full of light,
it's the most convivial room in the house.

I buy a dishwasher. We call it Horatio.
It makes a difference to the midnight washing-up.

~

Otago's arts fellowships enrich Dunedin – each year three practitioners
add their gifts to the city's culture. Many stay – for instance Marilynn
Webb, who trained with Ralph under Gordon Tovey. They have a
similar way of integrating life and art – her story is woven in the south
from this time on.

~

He chants for me the Māori words of the Psalms.
I hear 'Te Tangi o te Pipiwhararoa', the poem given to McCahon,
in his soft voice, smoky, no edge to it.

~

Layer on layer of Ralph's works
cloak me.

Were I to lift them gently away with tweezers
in all their dark seductive textures,

might I find myself in my spare time
doing what, apart from appreciating, facilitating?

Sewing, cooking, knitting, spinning, reading,
acting, visiting, making jam, bottling fruit, baking bread ...

My focus was on him – his work intrigued me –
I was fortunate to take part.

~

Dunedin's new Fortune Theatre has its home in the Athenaeum.
The homosexual theme of the first production, *Fortune and Men's Eyes*,
is controversial. Ralph designs the set; prison bars of light and shadow.
In *The Lover* I learn the acute economy of Pinter,
the value of silence.
Admirably, I thought, in *The Two Tigers*,
Louise Petherbridge as Katherine Mansfield
did not wear an Egyptian-looking wig.

1975

I have a new job at St Hilda's, teaching English and French to junior
classes and French to senior students, whose oral work is advanced.
We discuss Camus and listen to Edith Piaf, Jacques Brel, Françoise
Hardy. I'm on the committee of the language teachers' association
and experiment successfully with audio-visual methods using tape
recorders, wanting to take the language out of the textbook into the
classroom.

In the room next to mine, satiny-voiced Marilyn teaches English.
Feminyms: my friends whose names are spelt differently but sound the
same: Marilyn and Marilynn, Marion and Marian.

~

Jack Body and Barry Margan use a range of mysterious instruments
in an improvisatory performance, 'Sound Movement Theatre', at Allen
Hall.

The written score for 'Song Cycle' is pictorial, circular,
arcane notations denoting varying states
of instrument and sound in time and space.
The musicians are on the floor of the hall;
the dancers, Char Hummel and John Casserley, on the stage.
In semi-darkness the composers
prowl around, making sound.

Ralph designs the set and costumes. He tries spray-painting leotards
but the dancers think it makes their bodies look too lumpy; he projects
instead onto bodies and backdrop some photographic slides he's
doctored with ink blots and scratches, casting patterns on the dancers,
changing as they move.

There isn't time to do what he'd prefer – a set of hanging banners
for John and Char to dance between.

~

Materials are always an expense.
I buy a bolt of canvas for the banners.
Ralph stretches them on long boards on trestles
on the kitchen lawn at Careys Bay, starts painting –
Oh no, here's the weather coming over – no time to take them in
like washing, they'll have to stay out
in the rain's
   serendipitous
     patterning

When they're dry he lays them out across the floor. We have our
favourites among Bill's words. Ralph doesn't integrate the text into
the main painting but gives it its own space on the unstretched canvas
at either end. He concentrates close up on the lettering. It's easy to
make a mistake transcribing poetry. A couple of times I am a useful
proofreader.

We hang the first 'Song Cycle' banner over the verandah
for Mike de Hamel to take a photo.

~

Barry Brickell stays at the studio, making pots. He's a most enjoyable
person. With his remarkable breath control he can give an excellent
impression of a steam engine tackling the gradient.
In the garden he builds a brick kiln with a lean-to corrugated iron roof.
He does a firing with gusto – shovelling fuel as the kiln heats up – and up –
while it's snowing –
I'm sitting on the roof
watching sparks rise into the sky
from which snowflakes come drifting
down onto my hand –

Then whoosh! a brilliant flare of gas up the chimney.

~

Outside the studio in a sale of Barry's work
our friends buy salt-glazed mugs, cups,
plates, terracotta jars and casserole dishes.
Barry and Ralph work together
with an optimistic, energy-exchanging attitude.

~

I audition for *Twelfth Night* at the Fortune.
Jan Prettejohns, the director, has a black leather coat, an electric blue silk
scarf and a wit I relate to at once. Sweet and sharp, she casts me as Viola,
with Alex Gilchrist as Sebastian. (We both have a gap between our front
teeth.)
Jan directs our rehearsals with energy and a sense of fun, choreographs a
spectacular slow-motion swordfight between me and Alex.
The wardrobe, designed by Murray Hutchinson, is a patchwork of rich
fabrics.
For Viola, he makes a boyish costume in velvet and brocade.

Sebastian and I look – sort of – similar, if you suspend your disbelief.
Shakespeare sharpens my mind – by the time the season starts
I know the whole play by heart.

~

In *Pathway to the Sea* Ian Wedde, living at Port Chalmers, gives early
warning of plans to build an aluminium smelter at Aramoana.
A cruel idea to blanket with concrete this fertile wetland at the
harbour heads.

~

We are opposed to the atmospheric and under-atoll
nuclear testing in the Pacific.
Mururoa.
Fallout.

~

Early evening. The sounds of insects
are as clear cut as the silhouettes of the hills
around me. I put pencil-tip to paper,
draw the melodies the hills sing,
with attention to incidental sounds.
Looking across the harbour to Taiaroa Head
I watch the last sun leave the last beach,
Te Rauone, unaware
that a couple more turns of the stair
and I'll live there a while
on the edge of the channel,
nestled in sandhills and seagrass.

1976

Symmetry, harmony, all lines graceful to the eye,
 our house at Careys Bay is an artist's house.
There's no separation between art and life.
With Ralph's acrylics Andrea paints a mural for the bathroom,
Princess Marina from the TV series *Stingray*,
'Anything can happen in the next half-hour.'

The house was once a convalescent home for patients who came from
Dunedin to benefit from the sea air. Later, it was divided into upstairs
and downstairs flats, the connecting stairs closed off. We tap the
walls and floor, remove boards, revealing the original kauri staircase,
balustrade and all. The house seems to open up and breathe.
We lie awake, hearing ghosts whispering up and down the stairs
all night, clearing out.

~

Donald Reid, bachelor, in a cream sportscoat, a rosebud (Cécile
Brunner) on the lapel, as debonair as Maurice Chevalier but without
the French, gives dinner parties at his house overlooking the fishing
boats in Careys Bay.

~

In her timber hut at Mahinerangi
Marilynn Webb draws the water, folds the hills,
shades the clouds over raw tussock land,
gives the landscape all her energy.
The landscape gives it back – I learn from her
to tap and to sustain this circuit.

~

Feeling the depth of Māoritanga in our life I go to evening classes in te
reo at Scott House, near the St David Street bridge. My grasp of syntax
isn't bad, my aural comprehension stronger than my speech. When

the course is over I speak it to myself, practise its patterns, wish Ralph
would speak to me – but he says it was beaten out of him at primary
school. Of course he knows it. I am a Pākehā schoolteacher and there's a
lot I don't understand.

Male poets give their words to Ralph – Hone, Ian, Bill. I look for poetry
by women for myself – Fleur Adcock, Janet Frame, Elizabeth Smither,
Lauris Edmond, Fiona Kidman, Rachel McAlpine, Jan Kemp.

Now and again I begin
to feel a poem condense and flow – catch it – tips of my fingers –

~

Ralph's 'Song Cycle' banners are exhibited
in the Bosshards' upstairs gallery in Princes Street.

Some people anxiously   seek   meaning, are frustrated,
some rejoice in   wonder
at sheer   felicity   of   small-scale   lacy shadows
seeming to   permeate   the canvas surface
of the moonlit banners   hanging
        quietly   singing poetry.

~

When Barry stays at the studio again
he achieves some serendipitous experiments,
decorates with hand-stamped lettering
his clay pots large and small.
I have a dear wee pot of his that fits
my cupped hands. He has impressed on it
greetings for me at Christmas 1976.

1977

I read and write beside the window in my study,
honeysuckle and jasmine above the garden gate.
My muse is Muriel, our pearl-grey cat.
Thinking of the double-slit experiment, I write 'Interference',
a poem in which she intervenes,
a sort of M-particle disrupting the wave function.

Educational jargon inspires my first poem in print,
'A Letter from The Department',
published by Lauris Edmond, poet, editor of the *PPTA Journal*.

~

Drinks at Rodney's – gin and vermouth,
brass ashtrays overflowing, discussion of the arts, the latest gossip.
Rodney's wit is wicked but his hospitality generous
to the artists and intellectuals in his Friday evening salon.

One evening I wear my orange jumpsuit
with cutaway shoulders and appliqué flowers.
'That girl, darling,' calls Eunoë Christie to Rodney piercingly
across the room, 'has absolutely no bottom.'

~

I absorb Chekhov's subtle psychology as Masha in *The Three Sisters,*
with Terry MacTavish and Sarah Delahunty,
directed by Jan Prettejohns.
I don't aim to be a professional actress – my pleasure now not so much
acting as interaction, participation in a play brought to life.

~

With fierce concentration Ralph's working on the 'Godwit/Kuaka'
mural, a commission for the Auckland Airport,
tracing thousands of brilliant lacquer lines in subtle gradations, on
sleek black.

His spectral chord tone by tone
spins tunnelling towards the central panels, inscribed with words
above and below three circles.
As he writes the words on the central panels
he speaks them aloud – it's ancient Māori poetry.
Gives me the shivers.

We respect Ralph's work as if it were a senior member of the family.
It takes precedence.

~

I have to look carefully to find myself among all this.

~

Gradually I learn how to shape my inner language.
Writing is my daily occupation. At twenty-eight I seek the solitude I had
when I was young, in my deckchair in the garden,

take a thermos and a sandwich,
walk along the coast road towards Aramoana,
find a spot somewhere near Deborah Bay
from where to draw the peninsula hills,

rejoice
in the flow of thought from eye to pencil-tip,
mind skimming the edge of sense –

begin a
poem about the neural connection
between eye and ear and hand,
looking out for anything
'counter, original, spare, strange'.

~

Words Fail Me

Air's so clear it's tinged with black.
My favourite spot for looking at the
peninsula is on a headland above the road
to Aramoana. Here I sit in the sweet buttery
gorse, a tiny ringing cicada song coming
from many points in space. From the port
comes the logsnatchers' angry growling.
A single black shag on the water which is
pocked pale and darker blue pointilliste
and then the hill's limbs gracefully collapsed,
relaxing, stroked by the shadows of clouds.

It is all a continually moving
picture show. I get out my paper
pencils and ink not to copy nor to
describe but to put into line what
the words are not fluid enough for.

Well this is nice
under the sun on the
field in the grass.

I have this desire to sing
the peninsula. You can do it easily
in situ but for those miles away
you need a score. So I've been
drafting lines onto graph paper
and pairing coordinates. I hope
that they can then be mass produced
in the form of sheet music which
can be sung anywhere. It's a good
restful song today, fluent and
blurred by travelling clouds; occasionally
the tones deepen and the air is colder.
The sun is behind a cloud and the

sharp edge of Mopanui razors the blue
and white. This side's lines are deeper
and darker, bass and baritone; the hills
across the water are a soprano fairytale
in counterpoint. Words
                              fail me she says
and proceeds to fill several more lines
with scribbled black biro words fail me

~

Dad keeps the manuscript autobiographies of his forefathers in his roll-topped desk. We talk about our old St Kilda: Hirta the island, the street in Village Bay where his family's stone house stood – still stands, partially; when they departed for Australia it was kept for them just as they'd left it, in case of their return.

Callum travelled as a young man
from St Kilda to Melbourne in 1852
with his father Finlay and his mother Christina
on the good ship *Priscilla.*
Christina, having lost her eldest daughter Rachel
to measles on the voyage, was widowed
shortly after they arrived – old Finlay pined for his island.
She lived in Gaelic Town with Callum, who found work
making bricks and planting market gardens.

Teen, her granddaughter, never married
but cared for Callum Mor when Mary died.
The old man in his Tam o' Shanter shouted, 'Strupach!'
banging on the floor with his stick
and his daughter appeared
with piping hot oatcakes.
Teen's brother Finlay worked in market gardens
then joined the Railways, where in the guard's van
he studied Hebrew, Latin and Greek

to become a Presbyterian minister.
He was Dad's grandfather.

St Kilda and its history are a rich poetic source.
On the verandah at Careys Bay after a morning
collecting mussels, walking on the beach
thinking of ancestors, I close my eyes;
imagine myself a woman of Hirta standing atop a cliff,
looking out to sea and down through layers
of wheeling seabirds
to the thin white line at its black foot.
Lonely – I in this country, my man on that island
across the water too wild to cross –
I feel it in my bones, writing 'Songs for a Far Island'.

~

On Mum's side, Granville Sharp
was pretty good at Greek as well,
his contribution to Greek scholarship being
his Rule, a grammatical principle
which operates, many say, without exception.

~

A pink geranium climbs the rimu wall
beside the leadlight kitchen window.
On the sideboard a vase of tall white daisies,
books, cookbooks, magazines, an electric drill,
paint pots, brushes, wine bottles, glasses.
Shelves of plates, cups, bowls, goblets,
paintings, drawings, prints, etchings on the walls,
on every surface sculptures and pottery
all New Zealand art; a potent aesthetic space.

The kitchen's full of laughter and conversation
with visiting friends, artists, writers – mainly men

doing the talking. Twenty years younger than most,
I cook and listen. I'm making coffee after lunch one day
when somebody says, Hey, wish I had one of those –
referring to me –

I note this; refrain from answering back
because I'm colouring inside the lines
as wife, mother, teacher among intelligent colleagues
including my mum, doing some theatre,
keeping house, gardening, entertaining.
Not until my creativity
demanded self-determination
was this happy state disrupted.

~

The family's coming for Christmas dinner. Ralph bones the turkey,
I make a stuffing of veal, pork, chicken livers, cognac, nutmeg, black
pepper, eggs, herbs, garlic, spread it on the turkey on a piece of muslin,
roll and tie, simmer on a rack in the poaching kettle with *mirepoix* and
stock. A memorable *galantine*.

Snow on Christmas Day – in midsummer –
reminds Mum of her English childhood.
We light fires, light candles, pull crackers,
tell jokes, wear paper hats, drink wine,
draw the curtains, hush the laughter
while Dad lights the pudding, ghostly blue
flickering brandy flame.

~

Granny's lorgnette, like Bo-Peep, has survived the journey of my life.
It is of silver-plated steel, fine blue enamelled decoration on the handle.
At the touch of a thumb, one lens becomes two.

Interposing the lens between my eye
and the computer screen
and taking it away again,
I'm reminded of Mr Fairmaid the optometrist
testing my eyes for new glasses
with an array of lenses. Now tell me, Priscilla,
which way is better, this way (switch)
or this way? This (switch)
or the other?

~

I'm halfway between a straightforward French teacher and something
else. I don't know what it is. It's not an actor but a new part of my
personality, asking to be heard. Sometimes I feel like the Ugly Duckling
surrounded by the lovely swans of art.

~

While we were in rehearsal for *The Three Sisters*
I dreamed myself standing in the wings of the Regent Theatre
in the blackout, about to go on stage.
I realised that I was expected to deliver a reading of New Zealand poetry
but didn't know any – didn't have a script –
I'd have to improvise the whole thing on the spot.

A sticky situation, alone in the dark.
A leap of faith required.
A signal dream that I was to be a poet?

1978

Ralph's keen to go to Europe again and look at art. It's time to refresh my
French. Andrea's at a good age to travel. He applies to the Arts Council
for funding; I take a year's leave from St Hilda's.

Three zip-up camping bags, yellow, red, green,
tickets, passports, money,
leapfrog to London via as many art galleries as possible.

In memory, over time,
scant glimpses eclipse surrounding detail.

Hong Kong window, a zigzag hillside path,
a slow-motion Tai Chi ballet,
each private person inward turning.

Istanbul hotel, men in dark suits, upholstered chairs,
a figured carpet, polished tables, velvet curtains.
Blue smoke in a horizontal layer. Ears open to unknown language.

Jan McConnell walks into a bar in Athens, dramatic in a yellow caftan.
We acted together in *Lysistrata*; now she and Ray Snowden live
in the cluster of antique dwellings on the hillside below the Parthenon.

Acropolis marble electric underfoot.
I see for myself the caryatids,
graceful and aloof, like school prefects.

Rome, Pensione Erdarelli. Ralph's eloquent sign-language charms the
landlady. He draws her portrait, is abundantly provided with chianti.
A memory persists like a short film – I come into the room, Ralph is
sitting in the shadow, she's in the light, laughing open-mouthed, in
delight.

Jack Hotere's grave at the Sangro cemetery. We leave on the gravestone a rosary sent from Mitimiti. Silvery olive leaves whisper a prayer.

Madrid, muted echoes, feet on stone. While we walk around the city Ralph sketches 'Window in Spain' drawings, finishing them at night in the hotel room. We spend hours in the Prado. I'm riveted by Goya, blazing light in black. Ralph's deep into Rembrandt. Andrea vows she will return to Velázquez.

~

Trafalgar Square pigeons, ancient churches, bridges, ladybird-red double-deckers, multi-layered history; a feeling that I have lived here before – or someone very like me, perhaps in Zoffany's portrait of the Sharp family?

In the National Portrait Gallery, an eighteenth-century musical party: fifteen people and a dog crammed into the painting with their instruments, playing chamber music on the barge *Apollo*, floating down the Thames.

The tableau is contrived, its structure triangular; the orchestra disposed between William Sharp, beside the mast at the top of the canvas, and the family dog, lying at the bottom. Below William, Catherine, his wife, holds their daughter on her knee. Foremothers, my bones.

Granville Sharp, philanthropist and abolitionist, leans across the harpsichord, sheet music in one hand, flageolets in the other. He and William notably took up the cause of the slave Jonathan Strong, and helped him to freedom.

~

I'm invited to be one of the readers at an evening of poetry and music at New Zealand House. Michael Houstoun plays the piano and Jane Waddell, Alannah O'Sullivan and I read a selection of New Zealand poetry. I choose to read a poem by Kevin Ireland – to my surprise he's here – he speaks to me – he's good-looking, with dark-framed glasses, wavy dark hair – I hadn't imagined him alive and in London.

~

We name our red Escort stationwagon Vanessa Red,
having recognised Vanessa Redgrave crossing the street,
tall and lean in a tawny crocheted beret.

We cross the channel by hovercraft, get used to driving on the right and follow the map to Luzé, in the Loire valley. The *gîte* in an ancient farmhouse has two rooms, white-washed walls, wooden furniture, gas for cooking and hot water, a simple kitchen opening on to the farmhouse courtyard. Each day we visit a château. I'm collecting pamphlets, tickets, tapes, ephemera to use for teaching. Mme Fouquet speaks no English. Ralph swaps a pencil portrait for her antique wall-clock. So we travel around with a French farmhouse clock in the back of Vanessa Red.

~

In Avignon my ear is tested by the accent of the Midi
but after competition with a German gentleman
I negotiate to rent Ma Villa, on the Ile de la Barthelasse
in the middle of the Rhône, close to the old Pont d'Avignon.
In a pale dry garden of summer grass, Ma Villa is a pretty house,
white roughcast with an orange tile roof.
We spend most of the time in the leafy shade of a tonnelle
above a long table covered with an oilcloth, where Andrea and I
read and write in wavering patches of light and shadow
while Ralph paints in his open-air studio, set up under an apricot tree.

Friends on holiday visit: Sean and Helen Comyn, Michael Houstoun, Paul Richardson, Jane Waddell, Ivan Wirepa. We make trips to market, to the Palais des Papes, to Roussillon, Orange, the Pont du Gard, Les-Saintes-Maries-de-la-Mer, the Camargue, visit ancient monuments, see

art, drink rosé, pastis, cook on the barbecue, play pétanque,
laze in the sun.

In the Place de la Poste
at a café table under a tree
I get a white-out from a pigeon,
right on my head. Am I lucky?

In Avignon I began to write seriously. It was a pleasure and became a
necessity to put our experiences and surroundings into words. I looked
forward to the time each evening when I would continue writing. It was
my Katherine Mansfield moment – later, because I'd had this happy
time in the south of France, I didn't regret my decision, after the *Rainbow
Warrior* bombing, not to go back teaching French nor to apply for the
Katherine Mansfield Fellowship in Menton, thereby shooting myself in
the foot in a literary way, in a silent protest of one.

~

At Les-Saintes-Maries-de-la-Mer
I cross a gypsy's palm with silver.
She takes my hand and tells me in her accent of the Midi
speaking rapidly, wide-eyed,
Ah *Madame*, you have travel, many changes
and marriage to come. I laugh that I'm married already
and she laughs too, her golden skin creased
in merry wrinkles.

~

While we were in Avignon the Pope died.
Ralph used the newspaper headline for a painting, *Le Pape Est Mort*.
Not long afterwards, the new Pope also died.
We saw the headline in a Spanish newspaper – another painting –
El Papa Ha Muerto.

In Menorca we stayed with Sebastian Black and Judith Binney at
Binisafua. Now as I write, seeking the memory of Judy, she comes,
smiling, in a striped sundress down the steps to greet us.
We've brought the last of the figs from Avignon in an earthenware jar
filled up with cognac. In the whitewashed courtyard, in the white
sunlight, Ralph paints in white. The canvas flares.

~

Rodin
beyond sense
eyes can't tell me
touch can't tell me
marble's edge

~

A conversation about art with Billy Apple,
in a bar at Euston Station.
Later, in Dunedin, I wasn't surprised to see
that Billy Apple had painted the central pillar
of the elegant white Bosshard Gallery
uncompromising, brilliant red.

1979

Clean air; sea-sound; birdsong; poplar; jasmine; kōwhai; tall white
daisy; the harbour changing all the time through blue and grey and
sandy gold; the fishing boats; the welcoming house; the night sky; stars
in familiar places; Southern Cross and the Milky Way – Hone wrote a
poem to Andrea once about sky-kittens lapping up the milk up there.
On the verandah, at home in the southern hemisphere,
I watch at dusk two fishing boats coming in to Careys Bay
and write a poem, 'Homing In'.

~

Ralph has found a potential new studio at Port Chalmers,
on Observation Point at the top of Aurora Terrace, past Bully Hayes'
flagpole.
It's a ramshackle shed, the original stables of a large bluestone house
destined for demolition by the Harbour Board.
Under tall blue gums, looking out towards Aramoana,
this new studio will be spacious and light.

~

He paints three very long banners
of Hone's poem, 'Rain',
profound accompaniment to the poet's voice.

They are displayed in the tall lightwell of the newly built Hocken
building.
Viewed from the ground-floor foyer they look like a triple waterfall.

~

My classroom has a window over Dunedin and the harbour. It's
decorated with posters brought back from France, of Avignon, Paris, the
Pont du Gard, wild horses of the Camargue, fields of lavender. We have a
pay rise; I spend mine on a class set of audio-visual textbooks, *Nos Amis*.

~

My pen's a wand I dip into a magic liquid –
memories stream out like bubbles on a breath.

~

9 a.m. in the school hall with my English class, in a sea of blue uniforms,
listening with delight to living poets speaking their own words:
Sam Hunt, Hone Tuwhare, Alistair Campbell, Jan Kemp.

When Andrea and I come home from school she does homework, I do housework, make dinner, mark exercise books, prepare lessons. Then I start my other work – writing, drawing, catching thought – no easy trickling of the keyboard but pages of handwriting in notebooks, on envelopes and scraps of paper that arrive at the typewriter to be typed, without mistakes.

I write 'Timepiece'. Mum suggests I send it to the *Listener*.
They publish it; I'm shy to see my poem in print and visible to everyone.

~

Timepiece

I got home from work & looked at
my watch, & it said
Ten to five, so I did the washing &
picked some greens & tidied up the
kitchen, & sat down & had a cup of coffee,
& looked at my watch & still it said
Ten to five, so I did some ironing &
made the beds & thought Hell I might
get all the housework done in one day
for a change, then looked at my watch
but nope, no change, & I turned on the
radio & it said Ten to five, so
I cleaned the bathroom like mad &
picked some flowers & wrote some
letters & some cheques & scrubbed
the kitchen floor & got started on the
windows – by this time I was getting a bit
desperate I can tell you, I was thinking
alternately Yay! soon there'll be no more to
do & I'll be free, & Jeez what if I
RUN OUT? I did in fact run out, & out,
& out, past the church clock saying

Ten to five & the cat on the corner with
big green eyes ticking away, & up into the
sky past the telephone wires, &
up into the blue, watchless, matchless, timeless
cloud-curtains, where I hide, &
it is silent, silent.

~

Joanna Paul   Beta Street   kitchen table
window behind her   washing on the line
white winter   light   cast   down eyes
eyelashes   brushes   paints   shadows
sepia, indigo, pale blue   spare
space, bare   paper   water   colour
fields   disclose   a glimpse of her

~

Marilynn Webb in her studio
long dark hair centre parted
lips solemn   press, impress
a graven landscape   line in ink   a calm
mindprint, handprint

~

With Ralph and Andrea in the kitchen, our familiar drifting
conversation, fresh bread on the kauri table, cheese, wine, olives. Red-
gold walls and ceiling, scent of linseed oil, white light from the skylight
above us, the French clock from Luzé on the wall. On the brick step one
of the exploded amphorae Barry made, coiling clay rope, fired until
they split like terracotta fruit.

1980

In the dining room above the marble fireplace
McCahon's *Stations of the Cross* on hessian,
white numerals on black. A Woollaston landscape,
Ralph's portrait of Bet in shades of gold,
a brown and black *Sangro*, pale *Polaris*,
a Jeffrey Harris *Imogen* oil pastel,
Tony Fomison's *Head of Christ*.
On the mantelpiece a Greer Twiss sculpture,
elongated, supine red and blue legs.

Light hides in the dark brown velvet curtains
beside the window looking across the valley
at houses, back gardens, macrocarpas above
the graveyard, view framed by white iron lace.
The residents and artists are meeting
to discuss the smelter proposal.
Joanna will curate a protest exhibition.
Another group has declared
The Independent State of Aramoana.

I rip up the *National Geographic*, paste and collage resonant images,
write and draw over them using stamps, make a poem on a screen,
'Buffer Zones', which wins an anti-smelter poetry competition; carry on
with energetic collages over the study walls;
make a big mess with wallpaper paste, scrim, gold paint; write a
poem, 'Smelt', about an aluminium pressure cooker tortured beyond
endurance. Meltdown.
Meanwhile Andrea writes a protest letter to the Queen.

~

In local painter Jeffrey Harris's drawings, persistent memory
reinvents itself in pencil line as image, language
longing, terror. He's taciturn – shy, I think.

On the walls of the Frances Hodgkins Fellow's studio Andrew
Drummond projects slides of the tidal flats at Aramoana: snails, cockles,
seaweeds, wave-patterned sand, magnified to formidable scale. At Scott
House he gives a series of lectures on Marcel Duchamp that pique my
imagination, renew my taste for the Absurd.

Di Ffrench lives in Harbour Terrace. I go over for coffee,
find her perched on a ladder
focusing her zoom lens on a large white
bowl of water on the floor.
Stillness in the room
deep concentration.
Shutter click.
She's photographing the meniscus.
Developing interest in the skin of water.

Ralph paints 'Black Windows' in wooden sash window frames; on rusty
iron, 'Vive Aramoana'. In our house his work is the focus, especially in
the lead-up to exhibitions, making, choosing, signing, packing, sending,
deadlines, short fuse, exhibition frenzy, drinking coffee
laced with whisky.

1981

Early at Mahinerangi – calm and bright.
Everyone's still asleep but young Ben Webb. He and I
might be the only people in the world, on the shore
beside the tranquil lake. Here and there a blip, ripple –
trout rising. Looking more closely at the water we observe
myriad insects trampolining on the surface tension.

In the clarity of water, air, idea,
'To Ben, at the Lake' wrote itself
before breakfast. The idea of the meniscus joined
a little homily about living in this world. The poem
saddens me now, since Ben, a gifted artist,
has passed away.

~

In the Mozart Fellow's studio Chris Cree Brown opens an electronic
sound-garden to me – exhilarating synthesiser, tape recorders,
microphones – magic flowers –
shall we make a recording? My ears are rinsed with electronic sound,
I'm vitally interested –
what say
we add language?
I make a concrete poem with stamped words, black ink on paper,
'Crystallography'. We read it as a score for voices, record an
electroacoustic work.

I'm grateful to my friends the composers – Chris, Gillian Whitehead,
Anthony Ritchie, Jack Body, who taught me awareness of spacetime
and to focus my hearing.

In the entrance alcove of the pub
at the bottom of London Street, eyes closed,
concentrating inside my headphones,
taping on my Sony cassette recorder
the sounds of the Springbok Tour demonstration
coming along George Street,
I hear wind and rain.
The sounds are muffled – suddenly my alcove
is crowded with wet policemen.

~

The smelter again. To Ralph, it's political. With Ian's *Pathway to the Sea* in mind he paints some sheets of demolition roofing iron – a new surface – harder, weathered metal, rusty corrugated surface flicked with paint, spattered, tall shape of this ad hoc material, stencilled words, white splats, sea-foam or seagull, a wooden board nailed across the top to steady it. Lead-headed nails.

~

Frankton's changed. There's a small plain house with a stone patio where the two huts used to be. Dad doesn't believe in luxury in a holiday crib, but around us substantial houses have been built with names like 'Grande Vue' – with garages; shrubs and trees from the garden shop; even letterboxes.

The frog pond has disappeared. The schist and boulders of the bare hillside have been used in walls, terraces, fireplaces. Jet-boats slice the morning silence, bringing parties of water-skiers to the beach. It seems pretty crowded to us, who find Aramoana crowded if there's more than half a dozen people there.
Looking up at the Remarkables I write the poem 'Living Here'.

Queenstown is growing. On sunless
inhospitable slopes the motels burgeon.
The mountains gaze loftily over us, like caryatids.

~

At Observation Point, Anthony Stones
sculpts the head of Ralph in clay,
to be cast in bronze.
The uneven red brick floor in light and shadow,
form, shape, wild hair in the sculptor's hands.

~

With Martha Morseth, a colleague at St Hilda's, I organise a poetry reading series at the Fortune Theatre – microphone, café tables, cabaret atmosphere. Dunedin poets: Peter Olds, Brian Turner, Bill Sewell,

Joanna Paul, Sue Heap, Marion Jones, David Holmes, John Dickson, Graham Lindsay, John Gibb, David Eggleton, Liz Cooper, Kevin Cunningham, Alan Roddick, Hone Tuwhare, Jeffrey Harris, David George, Harry Solomon. I read from my folder of unpublished poems.

1982

Marilynn's hut at Mahinerangi among birch saplings,
upland tussock gold with violet shadows.
Tom Field and Ralph fish for trout from the dinghy,
Ben, Kezia Field and Andrea run on the shore, in silhouette
against the water's silver sheet abraded,
ruffled, darkened, striped by breeze.
Marilynn's planting irises. I write my thirty-third birthday poem
just as it happens, from its eve at Mahinerangi
through a midnight party with Lyn and Russell Moses,
continuing in the morning as the rain pours down
all day on the musical house of rain, rain on which
the words of my birthday are written
held for a moment   gone

~

Tactile pleasure of the sketchpad.
The more I draw, the more concise the line.

~

When Ralph hears of his father's death,
we pack up and drive to Mitimiti.
In this quiet marae and church
at the edge of the ocean
at the core of the world
I encounter Te Ao Māori.

We walk along the beach beside the dark-veiled hills.
He remembers when he was a child,
at the back of the dunes there stood a fine old wooden house
reduced to tatters by the weather, deserted, driftwood-silver,
where the children played out imaginary lives
in bare rooms echoing the sea beyond
shredded lace curtains, bare feet on sandy wood.

On the way home I write 'Tangi at Mitimiti'.

~

The brown manila folder on my desk can't take any more poems. I send it to the only publisher I know of, John McIndoe, and try to forget about it.
One morning as we're leaving for school the phone rings – John McIndoe would like to meet me. He likes my manuscript, would like to publish it. Could I design a cover? I take a sheet of plain white paper and with my rubber stamp set, title it *Homing In*.

~

My brother, Malcolm, suggests I go to an introductory computing course – evening classes at Arthur Street School, in the classroom where I first read *Oliver Twist*. Sounds like maths to me but I go, interested in learning something new – Go to, like Shakespeare, *Goto* the binary tree, go with the flow, bring home an elementary program printed out on a strip of paper like a shopping receipt.

~

Curious as to where my experiments will lead me, working in my study at home, I'm making several series of artist's books on art paper with stamps, pen and Indian ink, drawings and scores for imaginary music and voices. Joanna's also making artist's books. It's a personal way for us to publish poems, the lettering on paper a sort of visual onomatopoeia.

Doctor Fell, of Oxford, collected
rare 'Puncheons, Matrices and Moulds'.

Patricia and Kobi invite me to show my books at the Bosshard Gallery
in Dowling Street.'Words/Images' displays them on music stands, with
pencil drawings on the wall, printed poems on paper and hanging silks,
all lightweight, musical.

~

At the Empire Hotel, Graham Lindsay causes
a cast-iron bath to be hauled into the upstairs bar.
He reclines in the bath reading a long poem from a sheaf of manuscript.
This poetry reading is a Happening,
a random, appealing *acte gratuit.*

Out at night with Ralph and a bottle of whisky
doing some anti-smelter graffiti at Aramoana.
He throws a bucket of black paint all over a company sign,
I write in large handwriting all along a corrugated iron fence
with a spray-can: 'The Sweet Slag Song of Aramoana'.
I give him a word for his 'Black Windows': 'Aluminpolitik'.
By this time we are somewhat drunk.

1983

With little warning I have to fly to Wellington, stay in a hotel and wear
evening dress.
Homing In has been placed first equal in the Book Award for Poetry with
Allen Curnow, and has also won the Jessie Mackay Award for the Best
First Book of Poetry. Belatedly, having obeyed J.K. Baxter and read little
Curnow, I buy a copy of *You Will Know When You Get There.*

The prize money buys an exciting, expensive B77 Revox reel-to-reel tape recorder. Now to experiment with sound. The Revox is extremely heavy. I lug it into my study, put it on the bench, connect it all up, amplifier, headphones, microphones, speakers.

Departing from the canon of New Zealand poetry
(though scarcely knowing what it is)
I put on headphones and tape some poems
combined with the sounds of my life
what say
I take two microphones out to the verandah
and set them up on stands, record in stereo
the train coming past above the back garden.
The headphones are comfortable. Milled knobs
control the dials with sensitive flickering
needles, palely register the train
far away above Purakaunui then hitting the red
as the sound approaches; a blaring whistle,
bells at the crossing, fade to birdsong,
far voices, laughter, the sounds of the sea,
a fishing boat chugging out to the harbour heads.
Then play it all back and mix together
with my voice reading poems such as
'Weekend Sonnets, Careys Bay', my eyes on the hills,
birds, colours and clouds, shifting surfaces of water.
I like the slim black Nakamichi microphone
with a foam cover, for close vocals; the wires,
the inputs and outputs, its connectivity to me.
Inside the headphones the sound world shines, accessible.

~

I'm invited to exhibit at the Red Metro, a gallery set up by Brad Smith and Geoff Ruston in a house in Stuart Street. This makes me work even harder. I write a long poem, 'What's Going On' and make some tapes for a sonic background.

120

Be experimental? Okay, I like doing graffiti. I spraypaint a mural
of poetry on the carpark wall outside; in the gallery pin dozens of
drawings on Pinex sheets, with here and there bright yellow and blue
packets of Drive washing powder; sketches and scores for imaginary
music; landscapes for instruments and voice. I set up the Revox, use
the microphone, read 'What's Going On', mixing my voice in with the
background tapes I've made. I call the exhibition 'Imaginary Music'.

In a review in the *Otago Daily Times*
Peter Leech demolished my confidence;
I hadn't given any thought to critics.
Joanna's review in *Art New Zealand*
was less aggressive.

~

At the Nine Poets reading in Christchurch,
as I came off the stage Janet Frame quietly said,
'Well done, it is real poetry.'

~

One day in the garden, pulling ivy off the bluestone wall
of the railway embankment, I injure my back again.
Tugging at the old tough vine – something slips –
that sickening, gristly feeling.
The pain in my spine persists and worsens.
This increases my awareness of time pressing.

~

Treble voices, twinning notes, harmonic beating. I take some 'Imaginary
Music' scores to school, set up the Revox in the best acoustic space, the
chapel, conduct my English class in an improvised vocal interpretation.
It's filled with the energy of laughter at the chattering and trilling
sounds they see, that make them sing.

There's a 'Girls Can Do Anything'
bumper sticker on my car. To that enterprising young woman
I'd say now, 'Perhaps, my friend, it's worth a try.'

~

Draw what you see, smiles Joanna.
I'm making japonica jelly – cut a japonica apple
in half and draw its seeded core –
drawing this several times, feel the lightning
connection between my eye and hand.
In the company of creative women,
Joanna, Di, Marilynn, Adrienne, Jan,
I absorb their gentle feminist insistence.
Anna Caselberg is shy, yet she has a gift.
Gil Hanly patiently documents her era.

Cradling a teapot fresh from her kiln, Alison
brushes back her dark gold hair, rubs dried clay
from her shirt, warms me with her wide smile.
A sculptural grace in my sister's pottery, fine
intuition of volume and balance, inside and out.

1984

Reading my poems at Sydney University and at the Institute of
Technology, I'm nervous but remember to project my voice. Ralph's
setting up his work for the Sydney Biennale. We stay in Paddington
with Sam Neill.

A trip is arranged with archaeologists
to visit Mungo, an ancient site inland
beside an evaporated lake.

Where there was water once,
red sand yields frail white cockle shells
and a woman's eyebrow bone, 40,000 years old.

Dawn sky grape and ripe mango,
the desert dried blood, squiggles in the sand
where snakes passed in the night.
Ralph derives drawings
from the patterns of test drills
made in the ground by the archaeologists
for carbon dating.
I write 'Mungo'.

~

Postmodernism – early ripples of the digital tidal wave.
Graham suggests sending some poems to Alan Loney's
new *Parallax* magazine. On the cover he uses
my score, a 'Conversation in a Crowded Room'.
Those first issues of *Parallax* in the bookcase
at the Flounder Inn – once I could put my hand on them –
a lamp, a rocking chair –

This Orwellian year invites a change of viewpoint.
I wear overalls and henna my hair,
take a wider look at art, see the new work
of interesting artists like Bill Hammond, hear
the Chills, the start of the Dunedin sound,
the female band Look Blue Go Purple.
The Red Metro has an underground atmosphere.

Writing poems in a spirit of disobedience
I rejoice in Mike Pearce's perfect ear, listen
to his guitar, put words to music, dream of flying
out the skylight in the roof of the Art Gallery at Logan Park.

Adrienne Martyn takes my photo there.
The camera unnerves me.
In the portrait I have short dark hair, round glasses
bare feet, nail polish. Grey parachute-silk World War Two flying
overalls.

~

Suppressing a giggle during a school church service
I think up a poem, 'Revolution', inspired
by 'The Emperor's New Clothes',
write it in my journal while my class
is getting on with their work.

~

Handwriting through the years I filled up many journals.
It was a pity to farewell them in the end
but they were interfering with my memory.
The continuous verbalising of my thought
seemed to hamper ordinary recollection.
The journals made a pile my own height, five feet two inches tall.
It had got out of hand – writing moment by moment
in cafés, airports, Dunedin, England, France,
Careys Bay, Grange Street, America, Berlin –
I didn't re-read them because they were dross,
a present, now past, from which the poems had been extracted.

~

I think I have another book. It is different from *Homing In*, not serious
in tone, mainly performance pieces. At McIndoe's, Bill Sewell, poet and
editor, hardly cracks a smile, publishes *Anti Gravity*. I think the physics
in it is still valid. Might a book be an anomalous event, pop in and out of
existence?

~

I write the present moment, barely grasp
this process of perception and participation.
On the kitchen lawn it's breezy, willows hush
on the bank below the railway line, the bluestone
wall upholds the railway embankment, red plums
ripen, ready for bottling.
Birdsong, distant machinery.

Put words on paper. This intimate act.

~

Thinking far outside the square,
dissolve the boundaries between music and poetry,
explore the sound and silence of John Cage.

~

Vegetable Garden Poem (iv)

On this side of the house
there is no wind
the garden is warm   the broccoli
has turned into immense pale yellow
bouquets   and the spinach is going
to seed   the place zipped through
with cicadas and yellow and white stars
You know words have a lot
to answer for
*   when the subtle illusion*
of meaning slips away
*   this vegetable*
garden released from its designation
becomes a riot of architecture
carrots underground missile sites
thistles explosions cabbages immense
veiny roses
*   and overhead a creaky whirr*

of woodpigeon and bees
homing in on softly blue
sun through short staple
cloud
                    Now I am listening very carefully
to these new dialects of earth and air

~

Making a large artist's book, a score
for imaginary voices of 'Solstice',
I wonder, is my poetry good enough – is it worth it –
but how can I ever know except by doing it?
If girls can do anything I can listen to David Bowie,
Talking Heads, wear pink and purple and black leather,
sunglasses, punk hairdo, long black coat, fishnets, heels,
reinvent myself; speak my poems to Mike Pearce's guitar
in a performance piece we call 'Dream Acoustics'.
I say aloud the written text in the outward version of my inner voice.
In the poem 'Sweet as a Nutter', Dolores, a performance artist, my alter
ego, laments her double existence.

~

I'd like a sabbatical from teaching – time to myself
to explore artistic languages, to write.

Saturday morning in the Careys Bay kitchen,
clouds scudding across the skylight,
Matthew the dog snoozing on the floor.
Andrea's away riding her horse,
Ralph's playing golf at Sawyers Bay,
I'm making bread – yeast dough rising,
flour heaped in the brown Brickell bowl,
warped as if it has been hugged before its firing.
Pink Floyd is turned up loud.

Beautiful things all around – the house replete
with art, the studios, the view, the visitors.
Sometimes it seems to me the art world
contains but few true thinkers
and many hangers-on.

~

A camera crew comes to make a documentary for *Kaleidoscope*. I read
'Timepiece' at the kitchen table while making sandwiches at the
suggestion of the producer.
Invited to experiment, I take the opportunity to throw a whole bolt of
white silk off the top of the Hocken building. They film it ribboning
down almost to the ground but not quite, because a few yards have
been cut off it to make some silk banners hung on bamboo, patterned in
pencil with phrases of poetry stencilled on imaginary landscapes.

Watching this documentary I see myself
a figment of electronic memory
from another viewpoint. It's like hearing myself on tape
for the first time, my perception mediated by technology.

~

Now the old stables are a spacious studio
with the original red brick floor, wavy in parts,
the old roof beams, recycled wood and windows,
pot-belly stove, areas to draw and paint in, each
with character and symmetry, a different quality of light.
Saw benches, power tools, stacks of materials, paint pots,
under the tall blue gums on the headland.

Ralph's in his maturity as an artist. His magnetism attracts other artists
who come to work with him. Chris Booth and Shona Rapira create
substantial sculptures; Patrick Power sings there; writers, sculptors,
singers arrive.

~

Meanwhile at home, in a letter from the Town Clerk, we're notified of the continuing demolition plans for Observation Point. Unrepentant about the plumbing and electricity, Ralph's building for privacy a high fence stencilled with protest graffiti.

Marti Friedlander photographs him working with a grinding blade on stainless steel beside the barricade. Up in the loft, I write at the window under the blue gums above the harbour. I look up at her inquisitive lens.

I write 'Baby Iron' while Ralph's exploring
shimmering mini-corrugations.

Fugitive lyric – we love, but a balance
is undoing, something like this change
from sheepskin polishing disk to sanding
disk to hard-toothed cutting disk to blow-torch
flame, distorting steel – playing merry hell with
the reflections.
     We're like Bill's 'Wulf' poem,
'You on that island
       I on this other.'

~

The Christchurch Arts Festival invites me to read, paying expenses and a fee. At this event I find that I can live inside my poems as I did when writing them, for the duration of their telling. In this sense, I find performance a recreation.

Martin Esslin, learned in Dada and the Absurd, invites me to breakfast in a courtly European way. We climb the Cathedral tower, stretch our eyes across the plains to snowy Southern Alps. He says, 'If ever you're in San Francisco ...'

This encouraged me, in my first year as Burns Fellow, to take up a
Fulbright grant, enabling our month-long colloquium at Stanford
University.

~

Surely performance poetry can make dramatic sense?
As in my Regent Theatre dream, I improvise.
Wacky language for the hell of it.
'Silly Thing', a rant about getting lost in a shopping mall, is published by
the *Listener*. There's some disquiet – Performance? The only other poet
who reads in pubs is Sam Hunt.

It seemed I'd cocked a snook at art. Such meanings people find – they
take exception – Rodney found me dreadful; Pat France cut me dead in
the Robbie Burns bottle shop.

Indeed, it was an exaggeration.
The Molotov cocktail was a fiction.

~

I'm getting tired, need time
for a couple of extra lives, can't hear
myself think – imagine I have to choose –
wonder now, couldn't I have managed both?

But Ralph's work was all-encompassing, somehow.

~

There is the problem of my back.
I am in pain. Just get on with it.

Breaking out of the gilded cage of myself,
determined to concentrate on my work,
I apply for the Robert Burns Fellowship.

~

Down by the Crescent Hotel
on the rocky shore at Careys Bay
I'm drawing Ralph and Andrea
in the red boat preparing to go fishing.
Their voices travel to me on the still air,
the water calm, on its unbroken surface licorice
and moonstone reflections wobbling under the hulls
of fishing boats, the ropes and nets all kissed with sparkles,
gently moving – feel intensely the reality
of sky and sea, red boat, figures in light.

~

I'm invited to Gore to read at the Eastern Southland Gallery
and perform in a Festival Cabaret.
There's a real sound system, lights – live music – spoken words
with their interior rhymes and rhythms lend themselves
to jamming with alert, intuitive musicians –
my poem,
which has begun in silence,
assumes an aural shape and cadence
in the manner of a song,
transferable to other minds
by means of voice.

~

I trade in my Daihatsu for a Fiat 124
midnight blue and silver
with a throaty growl – turns out
a liability but inspires 'Bad Bananas'
as I drive between Port Chalmers and Dunedin,
seeing Moon River's feathery magenta hair,
Buddy Fontana as that teddy-boy in the Roslyn Milkbar
who winked at me.

~

It was naïve to expect to write full time
and keep our household going as usual. I've dropped
and shattered a glass jar of spaghetti, scattered
all over the floor like pickup sticks.

Ralph drums his fingers on the table.
Andrea quietly makes cups of tea.

'Go for it, Mum,' she says,
'Be a writer. We'll be okay.'

~

It isn't easy   the poem requires me
to make available a private space
where   not   to think
but allow myself
to float in language
as if it were water   listen
a poet needs   her dreamtime

~

I'm invited to choreograph a short piece for the New Zealand Ballet.
Prepare music, fly to Wellington.
Think up 'Just in Time'.
Make a sound-collage on the Revox
with splicing block and blade,
out of fragments and passages of sound,
a speech by J.F. Kennedy, radio
commentaries from the Springbok Tour,
train sounds, natural sounds.
Choose eight dancers – racehorses –
high nervous energy – we improvise; develop
a remarkable ballet involving nurses, soldiers

and a dying swan.
But how on earth to end it?
what say
racks of billowing tulle, lace,
bolts of satin, ironing boards, wigs,
cloaks, uniforms, dressmaker's models,
a ballerina being fitted for a costume
posed on a chair like Coppelia.
With the help of the wardrobe mistress
the dancers sport leopard-skin leotards,
and a gorilla suit solves my problem – in the end
the dying swan gets carried off by the gorilla.
She has extra feathers down the front of her tutu.
He tears out handfuls as he lurches off the stage.

~

Resigning from school at the end of the year
I walk through a *Door That Wasn't There*
into my new office in the English Department
At Otago University.

A window. Bare shelves. A table.
A chair. A ream of paper.
A huge Imperial typewriter.

Close to the university,
31 Grange Street is a warm, brick
third-little-pig house
with a garden shed, a brick patio
and a kowhai tree. Here, I think
I can concentrate
as Robert Burns Fellow.

~

Nervous, half myself –
the other half's at home
in the silken wood, the skylight,
lace-edged verandah, train,
crossing bells, birdsong,
curved bluestone wall,
patio of bricks from the old
Love Construction Company
and my dear ones to whom
I give to understand
I'll not be far away –

I took little with me, but my red writing desk,
slipped out of the house for a while.

~

Musée Rodin

In the formal garden of the Musée Rodin,
as if through mist, a woman's face

Expressed in a material so fine and clear
it seems dissolving,

Unfocused, indefinable,
at one point marble, at another, air.

In transitional space between
one and minus one, outside and in,

She shimmers – her features blurred,
veiled, provisional, just out of reach,

In marble soft as human skin –
warm, permeable, bound to time.

Publication history for poems appearing in this memoir:

'Learning to Read', published in *Wild Sweets* (Dunedin: McIndoe, 1986) and *Axis* (Dunedin: Otago University Press, 2001).

'About a Singer', unpublished.

'Kids on the Road', published in *Anti Gravity* (Dunedin: McIndoe, 1984) and *Axis* (Dunedin: Otago University Press, 2001).

'Words Fail Me', published in *Homing In* (Dunedin: McIndoe, 1982) and *Axis* (Dunedin: Otago University Press, 2001).

'Timepiece', published in *Homing In* (Dunedin: McIndoe 1982).

'Vegetable Garden Poem iv', published in *Anti Gravity* (Dunedin: McIndoe, 1984) and *Axis* (Dunedin: Otago University Press, 2001).

'Musée Rodin', published in *Percutio Magazine* (Paris/Dunedin: 2012).